RUNNING
WITH
MAN'S
BEST
FRIEND

RUNNING
WITH
MAN'S
BEST
FRIEND

Davia Anne Gallup

Illustrated by

Kim C. White

1986
Alpine Publications, Inc.

Credits

Design and layout: Katie Mitchusson
Typesetting: Hope Guin, Artline
Cover Photos of Davia Gallup: E. Joe Deering

First Edition
First Printing February 1986

Library of Congress Catalog No. 85-52454
ISBN No. 0-931866-25-1

Printed in the United States of America.

To John and Willie

ACKNOWLEDGMENTS

I wish to offer special thanks to veterinarians Dr. Robert O. Shannon, Executive Director, Houston SPCA and Pet Columnist for the *Houston Post* and Dr. Anthony Meyer, 1984 Harris County Veterinary Medical Association President and a runner, for their knowledge and sensitive advice. I also wish to thank the following individuals for their help and advice: Dr. John W. Henley, DVM; Dr. Patricia Cooper, DVM; Phillip Snyder, Executive Director Tampa Humane Society; Joanne Schmidt, Publisher, *Inside Running Magazine;* Mark Scheid and Al Lawrence, co-authors of *The Self-Coached Runner;* my publisher, Betty McKinney, for her confidence and many useful suggestions; Rhona Schwartz for her fine editing work; and the many individuals who shared their dog jogging experiences with me.

And most of all, I thank John Hobbs for his patience, constant encouragement and loving support throughout this project.

CONTENTS

Before setting a 2:21:21 American record at the 1985 Chicago Marathon, Joan Benoit's running schedule frequently exceeded 120 miles per week. During hard training runs Creosote stayed behind, but when workouts were easy, he provided good company. (Photo by George Tiedemann)

FOREWORD

by Joan Benoit Samuelson
1984 Olympic Gold Medalist, Women's Marathon
and recipient of the Sullivan Award for Best Amateur Athlete 1985

Whenever my two-year-old Labrador, Creosote, joins me for a run, it makes for a great workout. We both benefit from the aerobic exercise and his playfulness often makes me laugh so hard that I almost have to stop running. Davia Gallup's book is a long-awaited guide for answering dog owners' questions about running with their dogs. Learning about another facet of their dog's captivating personality is just one more benefit readers will derive from this book.

Running with Creosote revealed two other things. The first is that residing in a small town won't prevent your dog from meeting his number one enemy—the automobile. Not long ago Creosote was hit by a car, an accident that made him no more the wiser about automobiles, but now he is reluctant to go near the scene of the accident. So until we reach the ever-changing, scenic backroads near our home in Freeport, Maine, Creosote stays on his leash at my side.

Second, as *Running With Man's Best Friend* recommends, a dog's running experience should progress gradually and be constantly monitored. Often Creosote runs up to five miles while I may only cover a mile. It seems nothing escapes his inquisitive retriever nose. I watch him closely and never let him get over exhausted.

Maybe Davia's next book will instruct dog owners on the pleasures of cross-country skiing with their dogs, another pastime Creosote and I enjoy.

The start of the Houston K-9 Fun Run. With up to 600 participants, it is the world's largest dog/owner race.

PREFACE

The idea of writing a book about training dogs to enjoy jogging began a number of years ago when my dog and I first started running together. Because she is a small dog (she only weighs twenty pounds), and was, at the time, what I considered to be a less-than-capable running partner, I had many questions about how to get her started on a running program. In seeking the answers, I discovered very little information was available and decided to research the subject myself.

During this time, I also noticed that many other people in the community enjoyed running with their dogs. This observation, combined with my research, lead to the creation of the Houston K-9 Fun Run, a two-mile race exclusively for owners and their dogs. The term "race" is somewhat misleading, however, because the event is actually more of a "happening" than a competitive race.

First held in June of 1982, the Houston K-9 Fun Run attracted just over 100 dog/owner teams, who were mostly personal friends and neighbors. Today, the race attracts hundreds of dog/owner teams and is the largest event of its kind in the world. It also benefits a good cause, as each year proceeds go to the Houston Humane Society.

The growth of the Houston K-9 Fun Run gave me an opportunity to question more and more dog owners about their "dog jogging" activities. I also began collecting information from other dog owners around the nation. What I learned from these individuals was that many of them were as uncertain about their dog's running capabilities as I had been. It was at this point that I decided to put my research to good use and write this book. So, just as Jim Fixx's *Complete Book of Running* served as an invaluable guide to joggers during the late 1970s, I hope *Running With Man's Best Friend* will serve dog owners in the same manner.

Davia Gallup
Houston, Texas

Chapter 1

RUNNING WITH YOUR DOG: THE NEW FITNESS PHENOMENON

For the last six years, Sheryl Seacat's most dependable running companion has been her loyal Labrador Retriever, Dayton. They are a familiar sight in their San Francisco neighborhood as they jog toward Lake Merced, their favorite running spot. The five-year-old Dayton has little trouble keeping pace with Sheryl, running an average of two miles a day, five times per week. Besides companionship, Dayton offers Sheryl protection; she knows that any dog, large or small, helps deter trouble.

Across the nation in Milwaukee, Wisconsin, Ken Williams enjoys running with his dogs, Kelly and Daisy. Kelly is a four-year-old Irish Setter that loves running and has a great tolerance for long distances. No matter what the weather, she's always anxious to run, averaging 50 miles per week. Daisy, on the other hand, is a four-year-old Labrador/Shepherd mixed-breed that comfortably runs shorter distances only a couple of times a week. Nevertheless, Ken has increased the endurance and improved the health of both his dogs, thanks to a regular exercise program.

Judy Warren is not a veteran runner like Sheryl and Ken. In fact, although this Los Angeles native had taken up jogging a number of times, she was not able to stick with it until she began running with her one-year-old purebred Cocker Spaniel, Chatsworth. Despite her own early failures at exercise, Judy knows it is the only way her pet can develop the muscle tone and definition so necessary for the show ring. With a minimum amount of running, Judy has managed to keep Chatsworth in prize-winning form and herself on a regular jogging program because she has both a companion and a purpose. Moreover, she has discovered that running with her dog is *fun*.

Running together is a pleasure both Sheryl Seacat and Dayton look forward to.

Sheryl, Ken and Judy are just a few of the many people who have discovered the pleasure of including "Fido" in a fitness program. With approximately 49 million dogs and an estimated 20 to 40 million joggers in the United States alone, it's no wonder that "dog jogging" is becoming more and more popular.

The phenomenon is a natural outgrowth of the fitness boom of the late 1970s. During that period, Americans were told by medical experts to change their sedentary lifestyles; the notion of "exercising your way to good health" was proposed and adopted. Since then, tens of thousands of Americans have integrated exercise, diet, and health awareness into their life. Advocates proclaiming the virtues of such activities as aerobics, swimming, yoga, running, or bicycling have no trouble finding receptive audiences. Fitness information has become so specialized that there are programs designed exclusively for men, women, children, working executives,

Accompanied by pets Kelly and Daisy, Ken Williams is never without companionship on his daily runs. Even below zero temperatures don't keep this trio from their sport.

and the elderly. In this vast exercise marketplace it is not surprising to find that man's most loyal and trusted friend — his dog — is finally being included.

WHY SHOULD YOUR DOG RUN?

There are many reasons for starting a running program with your dog, and you have possibly considered some of them. Running is good exercise; it helps your dog maintain or lose weight; improves muscle tone; builds endurance and a strong cardiovascular system; and, most of all, keeps dogs happy.

I discovered these benefits firsthand years ago after I adopted Willie (an unkempt white, shaggy Poodle/Terrier that looked suspiciously like Phyllis Diller) from the local humane society. I had been a solo jogger for a number of years and decided a dog would make good company on daily runs. I had a fairly good understanding of how regular running benefited humans, but as Willie became a jogger, I discovered that running is also good for dogs. Willie was nine months old when I started her on an exercise program, building her endurance and distance gradually. After six months, Willie was running 24 to 30 miles a week, acting lively and healthy, and looking forward to our runs together as much as I did.

During this same period I noticed my friends were constantly grumbling about their pets. They complained that their dogs were forever digging holes, barking excessively, and chewing everything in sight (a pair of my sandals included, the result of one unguarded moment while in a friend's home). For awhile, I actually thought something was wrong with my dog, not because she did any of the things my friends complained about, but rather, because she *didn't*. I began to wonder why Willie abstained from these typical canine antics.

My first thought was that my friends' pets suffered from boredom brought on by being left alone all day while their owners were at work. But Willie stayed home alone all day while I worked, so I dismissed boredom as the sole culprit. All the pets in question were adults, so I ruled out age. Then it finally occurred to me. The main difference between my dog and my friends' dogs was that Willie had an outlet for releasing pent-up energy . . . running.

Besides having a natural affinity for running, all dogs need to be active. Domesticated for at least 10,000 years, they have been bred to fulfill a number of services for humankind. Dogs have been used to herd sheep, hunt and retrieve game, pull sleds, and even fetch slippers. But because many modern dogs aren't called upon to perform such services, a large majority have become lazy, bored, overweight, and disobedient. Many are frustrated by lack of attention or interaction with humans. Or, in the words of author Winston Groom, they "have a lot of time on their paws."

Willie and I ran together usually in the early mornings. If my dog had any nervous energy, she undoubtedly released it through exercise. Running also provided an avenue for her to exercise her natural instinct to explore. There were always so many new smells, animals, people, and routes to investigate. A day at home was not imprisonment; instead, it was a time to relax.

Under-exercised dogs will often vent their energy in destructive ways by digging holes, barking or chewing excessively, or by displaying general hyperactivity. Pet authorities also believe disobedience, aggression, an inability to relate well to people, withdrawal, depression, and loss of appetite are other symptoms common to under-exercised dogs. What may appear to be a serious canine behavioral problem could, after all, only be "too much time on a dog's paws." Regular jogging can actually give pets a newfound purpose in life, and provide a time for bonding with their human companions.

RUNNING EXERCISES MORE THAN A DOG'S BODY

Understated in most popular get-in-shape programs is the notion that our "total self" (which includes man's mental, emotional, and physical well-being) can be developed through regular exercise. Not surprisingly, the need to exercise the "total animal" has not been fully recognized nor sufficiently emphasized.

The Weekend Dog, by Dr. Myrna Milani, is one of the few books which emphasizes exercising the total animal. Aside from a healthy body, she says, pets also need to have their minds and spirits exercised. Okay, I know you probably think this sounds a little too hip, "Like oh, wow, dogs can get it together totally." You ask, "What'll it be next, lovebeads for aggressive dogs?" Seriously, though, a running relationship is one of the best ways to exercise every part of your dog. By exercising the total animal, your dog's body, mind, and spirit are stimulated.

Dick Reeves, for example, a runner of eight years, recently included Morgan, his 20-pound Wirehaired Fox Terrier, in his running regimen. Although Dick runs 50-plus miles a week, Morgan averages 10 to 12 miles per week and never runs farther than 2 miles at a time. According to Dick, their frequent runs keep Morgan attentive, well-mannered, and in excellent condition. Dick probably never thought of these regular jogs together in terms of fulfilling Morgan's "total" needs, yet he has succeeded in doing just that.

Obviously, running exercises Morgan's body physically. Additionally, each jog through the neighborhood exercises his mind. For instance, a stop at a red light gives Dick an opportunity to issue training commands. He instructs Morgan to sit and wait. Once the signal changes, Dick then walks him across the street in the heel position. The dog responds to his commands willingly, and thus Dick has exercised his dog's mind as well as strengthened his spirit. Even a chat with a friend encountered along the way is an opportunity to build the dog's character. Morgan is instructed to sit and stay until the friend departs. Then the patient dog is released with a couple of "good boys," and he and Dick continue their run.

BORN TO RUN!

The great primitive cave artists often depict man with dog, and one can speculate that the two ran together and, subsequently, exercised together even then. When Og awoke in his cave, took his spear from Her-Og, and set out to bring home a dinosaur for supper, did he take trusty Dog-Og with him? Who is to know whether or not man's best friend ran with him out of need or just plain fun. Wouldn't it be surprising to learn that Dog-Og ran with Og for both reasons?

The origin of dog breeds of today can be traced to the Canidae family, one of the most physically active groups in the world. Comprised of coyotes, jackals, and foxes, the group also includes domestic dog's closest cousin — the wolf — an animal capable of roaming territory ranging from 30 to 200 miles and tracking prey for hours at a time. So while your pet no longer needs to hunt for his dinner, he still has the genes of his prey-chasing ancestors, animals built for quick bursts of speed and endurance.

But does ancestry alone make all canines qualified runners? It seems unlikely that a Dachshund or Cocker Spaniel is as well-suited for running as were their ancestors. The truth is, with proper conditioning, practically any dog can learn to jog, regardless of its size. For example, Jim Compton and Jon Levy, both Houston residents, jog with dogs so different in size and appearance that it's hard to believe they have the same roots.

Jim Compton has been running with his miniature long-haired Dachshunds for approximately two years, sometimes taking to the road with all *six* pets at a time. (Imagine coordinating six separate leashes!) Jim and his dogs manage it with ease, averaging three to nine miles per week. On occasion, Jacob Hydrocarbons, one of the better conditioned Dachshunds, runs six miles in one day with him. Jim says that one of the primary reasons he runs his dogs is to "avoid the weight and back problems" which Dachshunds can suffer.

On the other hand, Jon Levy's black Labrador, Buck, runs exactly the same distance he does, which is roughly 36 to 45 miles a week. Although Buck does nearly seven times the distance as Compton's dogs, both owners are able to enjoy running with their pets.

The more the merrier is Jim Compton's motto when he and his pack of Dachshunds go for a run.

Jon Levy's Labradors, Buck and Kate, have no difficulty keeping in stride.

Obviously, long-legged breeds such as Labradors, Dobermans, Retrievers, German Shepherds, and Dalmatians tend to make better long-distance running partners than, say, Dachshunds, Cockers, Schnauzers, and Terriers. Long-legged dogs have less trouble keeping stride with human runners, whereas smaller breeds have shorter strides, and must take more steps to keep up. Consequently, smaller breeds expend more energy and, in effect, run two to three times the distance that humans travel. But, as long as the mileage is compatible with the dog's size and he is in good health, he should be able to become a good running partner.

DOGS LOVE TO RUN

It's not unusual for dogs to learn the meaning of the word "run." Blu, an Australian Shepherd owned by Debbie Warner of Houston, Texas, is a perfect example. Whenever he hears this word he excitedly jumps up and down and barks nonstop until Debbi gets the message and takes him for a run. When Blu must stay behind — such as when the weather is too hot — he goes to the front window, pushes aside the curtains, and stations himself there while Debbi runs several loops around the block. As she runs past the window, Blu barks loudly to let her know he doesn't like to be left behind.

When asked why she likes to run with Blu, Debbi replies, "Companionship," but quickly adds, "and because he enjoys it so much."

Of the more than 150 dog joggers interviewed for this book, the question "Why do you like to run with your dog?" was answered with virtually 100 percent unanimity. The reply: "Because he or she loves to run." It's no wonder dogs love jogging. It usually increases the amount of time they spend with their owners and, as discussed previously, tends to make the animals calmer and more content. But, best of all, running strengthens the bond between humans and their pets.

Chapter 2

IS YOUR DOG READY TO RUN?

There are many questions dog owners should ask themselves before starting a running program for their pet. The five most important are:

What is your dog's physical condition?
How old is your dog?
What breed?
Does your dog know basic obedience commands?
Is your dog overweight?

The answers to these questions will help you determine whether your dog is ready to run (each question is thoroughly explained below). If all five questions are answered satisfactorily, your pet should be ready to begin jogging. Those of you who already run with your dog should review these factors to determine if your pet meets all criteria.

PHYSICAL CONDITION

To be certain of your dog's good health, visit a veterinarian for a complete *physical examination*. Discuss your dog's medical history with the veterinarian and explain your plans to start a running program for your dog. If your dog has any chronic ailments, diseases, or internal parasites, running may be too stressful.

It is important that your dog receive a negative diagnosis for heartworms before starting to run. Heartworms are a serious parasite, transmitted from dog to dog by infected mosquitoes. In southern states, where mosquitoes are active year-round, heartworm disease is a constant threat. As added protection against this disease, ask your veterinarian if your dog needs daily heartworm preventative medication and how often the pet should be tested for the presence of heartworm larvae. (Some veterinarians recommend testing for heartworm every six months.)

Booster vaccinations for rabies and other diseases such as distemper, hepatitis, parvovirus, leptospirosis, and parainfluenza are mandatory to keep your pet healthy. (Vaccines for the latter diseases are usually administered simultaneously.) Remember, the more your dog is out-of-doors the more he'll be exposed to infectious viruses.

AGE

Your dog's age will help you determine when it is safe to begin running. Keep in mind when referring to the following age standards that some breeds, such as German Shepherds and Irish Wolfhounds, mature slower than other breeds. Smaller breeds such as Terriers and Cocker Spaniels generally mature more quickly than larger breeds. The best exercise for puppies of any size or breed is free play with another dog or a person. Pups will usually stop when they get tired.

Here's a rule of thumb for deciding when to start running your dog:

Small breeds (approx. 1 to 45 lbs.) . . . . Over 8 months

Large breeds (approx. 45 to 95 lbs.) . . . . Over 1 year

Giant breeds (over 100 lbs.) . . . . Over 1-1/2 years

---

Of all the dogs surveyed for this book, Bali, a Doberman Pinscher, was one of the oldest dedicated joggers. His master, Paul Pena, remembers Bali's first introduction to exercise. Unlike most city dogs, Bali began his running career when he was a year old, chasing jackrabbits. Whenever he saw a rabbit he'd take off after it like a rocket. While in pursuit he'd spot another rabbit, change direction, and chase it. Eventually he had rabbits hopping around in all directions and didn't know which one to surprise next. Despite his determination, Bali never caught a rabbit. He did, however, manage to give himself quite a workout.

When Bali was two, he and Paul moved to Houston, Texas, and began jogging. Somehow, Paul always got the feeling that Bali thought their runs were hunting expeditions, because for the first mile or so he'd blast off, dragging his hapless owner along. By the time Bali turned eight, Paul knew that his "rocket-like" days were over and he'd have to go easy on him. From then on they never ran more than six or seven miles a week, spread out over three days. During warm weather they ran during the cooler morning hours. Bali had constant access to a wading pool, where he was encouraged to cool off after every run. Because he was in amazingly good shape, Bali ran until he died of natural causes at the age of ten.

Even at age ten, Paul Pena's dog, Bali, accompanied him on regular runs. Paul was careful not to overdo it and allowed Bali to rest when he wanted. (Photo by Joann Russell)

When running older dogs (eight years and older), it is most important to pay extra attention to their body movements. As with elderly people, older dogs can suffer from arthritis, rheumatism, and cardiopulmonary problems. When starting an older dog on a running program, go easy and be sure plenty of rest is offered. Don't be fooled by your dog's enthusiasm — over-exercising may put too much strain on the cardiovascular system and cause the animal to become ill or possibly even to collapse. An inability to keep pace with you, hard and fast breathing, and excessive panting are all signs that your dog may be overextending. If the animal is exhausted, carry it home — don't force him to do anything.

The old theory that each year of a dog's life is equivalent to seven human years has been abandoned by most animal experts. The dog/human age equivalent chart shown on page 14 is now recognized. Hence, a ten-year-old dog is equivalent to a fifty-six-year-old human. In other words, we can equate a one-year-old dog with the human adolescent and a two-year-old dog with the human adult. From that point on, the canine-to-human aging process levels off to a 1:4 ratio, with dogs aging about four times as fast as humans.

Dog/Human Age Chart

Dog Age	Human Age	Dog Age	Human Age
3 months	5 years	9 years	52 years
6 months	10 years	10 years	56 years
1 year	24 years	12 years	64 years
3 years	28 years	14 years	72 years
4 years	32 years	16 years	81 years
5 years	36 years	18 years	91 years
6 years	40 years	20 years	101 years
7 years	44 years	21 years	106 years
8 years	48 years		

One last note about running with an older dog. As dogs age, their immune system produces fewer and fewer disease-fighting cells, making them more susceptible to infection and illness. Therefore, it is important that they regularly visit the veterinarian to receive necessary vaccines, tests, and a physical examination.

BREED

Learn all you can about your dog's particular breed or mixed-breed characteristics, as exercise needs vary from one group to another. Some breeds (particularly those in the sporting, working, and hound groups) have high activity requirements which a regular running program could nicely accommodate. Others (mostly from the toy group) have low activity requirements. Most terriers, for example, possess high activity drives and require more outside activity. By contrast, a breed such as the Bulldog requires very little exercise. His build does not permit fast running, and his nose is not equipped for fast breathing. Furthermore, Bulldogs have extreme difficulty tolerating heat. Breed characteristics such as these are not the best attributes for jogging, and prior knowledge of them would definitely prevent future medical problems.

Learn the breed-related physical conditions to which your dog is prone. For instance, although the hereditary condition of hip dysplasia may affect all breeds of dogs, it is more common in such canines as retrievers and German Shepherds. Dogs with hip dysplasia (the degeneration and malformation of the hip joint which oftentimes results in arthritic conditions) should not be over-exercised.

The "Breed Profile Chart" in Chapter 4 suggests guidelines for how much running a particular breed can handle. These guidelines are based on each breed's particular characteristics and include other breed-related traits that dog joggers should know. Don't forget that these are recommendations only; no one knows your pet better than you and your veterinarian. The two of you can best evaluate your pet's capabilities.

KNOWLEDGE OF BASIC OBEDIENCE COMMANDS

Your dog should be well accustomed to a collar, leash, and "heel" work. He should respond to his name when called and be able to follow such basic commands as "No," "Heel," "Come," "Sit," "Stay" and "Down." While in motion, dogs tend to become excited; therefore, good dog manners are also important. Such manners simply mean that your dog is able to be restrained while around such distractions as other dogs, bicycles, people, and motorcycles and doesn't bark excessively or otherwise create a nuisance.

For those dogs with little knowledge of the basics, allow ten to twenty minutes before running (or allocate a portion of your run) for obedience training. If your dog doesn't understand what is expected, don't permit him to become frustrated; jog awhile and try again later. Always *be consistent* when issuing commands. The appendix at the back of this book, called "Obedience Basics," is a good source for this information, as are the many good obedience training books, such as *No Bad Dogs* (Summit Books, 1982) and *City Dog* (Dutton & Co., 1975). A particularly good training manual is *How To Be Your Dog's Best Friend,* by the Monks of New Skete (Little, Brown, 1978). If you're uncomfortable with the idea of starting your own obedience program, attend a good neighborhood obedience school. Be patient, never use corporal punishment, and praise your dog lavishly when it's justified. If you demonstrate interest and love, your dog will enjoy running with you, and the training process will be associated with "fun."

Every dog jogger I've talked with has at least one good story to tell about his or her pet's misconduct while running. Gail Sabanosh of Humble, Texas, an ocean drilling rig supervisor and owner of Curb E., an Airedale/ Shepherd mix, is certainly no exception. Her story presents a strong case for running with a dog that does what he is told. Furthermore, it illustrates the justification for having your dog on a leash while running.

Curb E. accompanies Gail just about everywhere, even on drilling rig assignments. Even days at sea don't interfere with their running plans — the pair still manages to jog about 25 miles a week. "Curb E. loves to chase anything on two or four legs," Gail says, "which usually doesn't present a problem because cats run up trees, rabbits are faster, field mice are too small to bother with, and birds fly away."

One morning while running, Gail noticed the telltale signs that Curb E. was about to go into action: her ears and right foot went up and her tail went straight. A moment later she took off at top speed. Gail, following at a run herself, soon discovered her dog's great interest — chickens! As she pursued Curb E. around a house, Gail's worst fears were realized.

Jogging with an unleashed dog invites trouble. Gail Sabanosh quickly discovered this when Curb E., her Airedale-mix, raided a chicken coop along their jogging route.

There her dog sat, dead chickens at her feet, chest puffed out and mouth full of feathers. Gail pleaded with Curb E. to come, but she ran around the other side of the house chasing yet another chicken. Then, as Gail looked up, she saw the proverbial man with a shotgun. Hurriedly she explained what had happened and begged him not to shoot either of them. The man agreed but admonished her to catch Curb E. Gail ran across the yard, over the fence, and into a ditch before finally tackling Curb E. in the middle of a huge puddle. After some disciplinary action, Curb E. was escorted back to the rig to receive what Gail says was the most severe punishment of all — not being allowed to finish the run.

Occasionally, even obedient dogs will misbehave. In my case, as a friend politely pointed out, it's not my dog's lack of knowledge that sometimes causes problems (she's a graduate of two obedience programs), but rather my lack of attention.

IS YOUR DOG OVERWEIGHT?

Lack of exercise and overfeeding are what usually cause dogs to become overweight. Dogs allowed plenty of exercise will keep trim all their lives. Starting a running program for the overweight dog can be hazardous because the excess fat puts a strain on the heart and results in poor circulation. If your dog is obese, ask a veterinarian about a reducing diet and begin with a walking program only.

Anne and Ron Grossman of Hopewell, New Jersey, were shocked when their veterinarian informed them that their precious Sherlock was overweight. When Sherlock, a Shepherd/Collie mix, was about four years old he began having trouble sleeping and breathing. One night he gasped for air so badly the Grossmans thought he was dying. The next day Sherlock visited his veterinarian and, after the Grossmans explained the syndrome of symptoms, they asked for a diagnosis. The veterinarian grabbed Sherlock by the fur on his rump and said simply, "Obese."

Anne's thoughts were, "I'm a Jazzercise instructor. I work out and diet to maintain my weight. My husband is a physician. We're both fitness-conscious individuals. How could we have overlooked our dog's need for weight control and exercise?"

Today, Sherlock is in great shape. Anne and Ron run him three or four times a week and he probably couldn't be healthier. Unfortunately, many dogs suffer weight problems. Owners need to keep in mind that dogs, like people, must eat less and exercise regularly to lose weight.

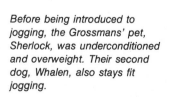

Before being introduced to jogging, the Grossmans' pet, Sherlock, was underconditioned and overweight. Their second dog, Whalen, also stays fit jogging.

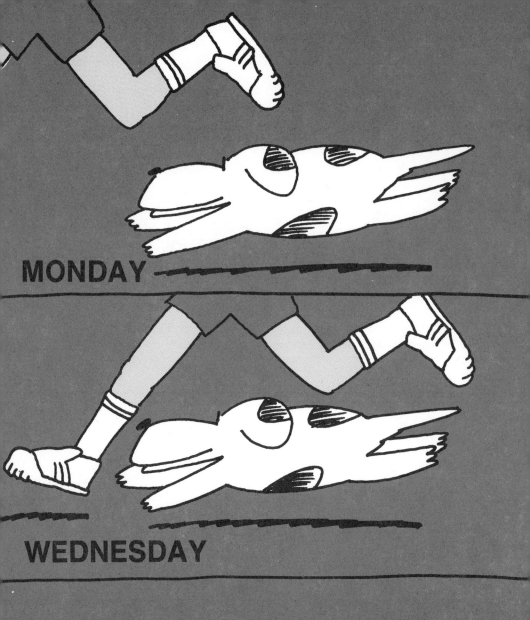

MONDAY

WEDNESDAY

FRIDAY

Chapter 3

GETTING STARTED: THE "3 x 20 EASY PLAN"

Getting your dog started on a running program probably seems simple. You put on your jogging shoes, get your dog's leash, and head out the door.

Unfortunately, dogs, like people, can get out of shape and it would be harmful to start such pets on a jogging program without proper preconditioning. Thus, borrowing a method used by lazy-at-heart masters, we now have a safe way to get house-bound hounds away from the hearth and out jogging.

This method is called the "3 x 20 Easy Plan." Simply put, the plan tells you how much, how long, and how fast to run your dog. Here's what it says:

Run at least 3 times a week

For a 20 minute period

At an easy pace .

Does this plan sound familiar? It's based on Dr. Kenneth Cooper's aerobic theory, formulated over two decades ago. Aerobic exercises such as swimming, bicycling, dancing, cross-country skiing and, of course, jogging keep us more physically fit than most other forms of exercise because they "promote the supply and use of oxygen," Cooper says. They also work our major muscle groups (i.e., thighs and buttocks) at a constant rate (which means hard but not too hard — about 70 percent of maximum capacity), for a specific length of time, and are ideal for keeping a person healthy. But what does oxygen supply and aerobics have to do with dog jogging?

You may be surprised to learn that your body and that of your pet are very much alike; in fact, there are far more similarities than differences. Moreover, when your dog runs, his body works the same way as yours. Therefore, aerobic exercise, especially jogging, is one of the best ways to keep people and dogs in shape.

Just like humans, dogs have a four-chambered heart that operates as a two-pump mechanism. Oxygen-depleted blood is received in the heart, then pumped through the lungs where it receives a new supply of oxygen, then returned to the heart to be pumped out to the muscles, tissues, and cells of the body. The essential ingredient to the blood-flow process is oxygen. During low activity a dog's heart and lungs maintain a steady rate of 80 to 100 beats and 10 to 30 breaths per minute. (By comparison, a low activity rate for a man is 70 to 80 beats and 15 to 18 breaths per minute.) As activity increases, more oxygen is demanded by a dog's muscles; his heart pumps harder and his blood pressure rises. Respiration (panting) also increases and can get as high as 300 breaths per minute. Incidentally, light pink gums indicate that your pet is getting enough oxygen. A blue or muddy-red tongue and gums may indicate a serious problem in the respiratory or cardiovascular system, and should be checked by a veterinarian. (Note: It's normal for Chows and Shar Peis to have blue or black tongues.)

With regular exercise the number of capillaries in the heart and skeletal muscles can actually multiply. Thus, even more oxygen can be taken in, which improves circulation, eases the heart's job of pumping blood to demanding muscles, and more efficiently removes waste products (such as carbon dioxide) from the body. To test how well your pet's heart and blood vessels are maintaining blood pressure, try this simple test: Press your finger against your dog's gums and then lift it away. The white area produced by the pressure should return to the normal pink color in one second.

I always thought of my dog, Willie, as just an ol' mutt. To know that her body works like mine and that physical exercise enables it to function better has given me a new appreciation for all dogs and helps me stick to a regular exercise program for her.

STARTING UP — DOGS

When first starting dogs on a running program don't overestimate their capabilities. Many of us believe our dogs are getting plenty of exercise during the day because they have a large enclosed yard or dog run. In reality,

if left to exercise on their own, most dogs — especially those that are overweight — will do very little except sniff around. Indoor pets even get less exercise, sometimes leaving their houses only to relieve themselves.

Start Gradually

To ease under-exercised pets (or owners) into a running program, start with a five- to ten-minute walk for the first few weeks. Then begin alternating two minutes of running with two minutes of walking for a period of twenty minutes. With practice, progress to four minutes of running, then eight minutes of running, and so on, until the dog is able to run continuously for twenty minutes. Remember: All dogs should start exercising gradually and be allowed to rest when they want to. If you have any questions about your dog's ability to begin a running program, consult your veterinarian.

Let time be your guide. Follow the "3 x 20 Easy Plan" for eight to ten weeks before increasing your distance. Most dogs should have little difficulty adjusting to this program as long as the pace is easy. An easy pace for your dog is one which he maintains comfortably — you may have to adjust your own pace or stride to achieve this result. Excessive panting, fast and hard breathing, and an inability to keep up indicate that the pace is too strenuous for your dog.

Before I adopted Willie from the animal shelter, I had started running on a more regular schedule, having become a "runner" instead of a "jogger." My intention was to get a big dog (or what I once called "a real dog") as a running companion. I believed that "the bigger the dog the better we could run together." As I soon learned, whatever Willie lacked in size, she more than made up for in exuberance.

To prepare Willie for her new, active lifestyle, I started her running by alternating walking with running. After a few weeks, her endurance increased. This gradual approach also gave her footpads time to build up and eventually she was able to complete a full loop around Memorial Park—approximately three miles. (Incidently, it may take more time to toughen up a dog's footpads than it takes to condition its body.) Today Willie averages 9 to 12 miles a week during the summer and approximately 24 to 30 miles in the winter.

To improve and maintain a level of fitness in both humans and dogs, the body must be given time to rebound. Therefore, it's essential that when you're starting out, you run your dog every other day, not on consecutive days. As your dog advances, follow the "hard-easy" theory of training that experienced human runners use: They believe that every hard day of running should be followed by at least one (preferably two) easy days.

If a busy work week interrupts your running schedule for more than a couple of days, don't worry. In five days only about one percent of your dog's aerobic conditioning will be lost. A steady dose of missed days isn't advised, but stopping periodically won't do any harm.

Incredibly fast, Francie Larrieu Smith of Austin, Texas, has held more than 30 American and world records. Shown running with Smitty, just one of two jogging Great Danes in the family, Francie's twenty years of running has made her a firm believer in jogging for dogs. (Photo by Sal A. Sessa / Courtesy Running Through Texas Magazine.)

Once your dog has built up strength and endurance (roughly two to three months into training) and is ready to advance, keep a mileage record. Do not exceed a ten percent mileage increase per week or run more than 25 to 35 miles per week. Keep in mind that for many owners and dogs, particularly smaller breeds, this distance is a lot to handle.

DETERMINING YOUR DOG'S LIMITS

By simple observation, I discovered my dog's comfortable running distance while visiting a friend's beach house. The house was located at the end of a four-mile farm road, which was always deserted because it was the off-season; therefore, I allowed Willie to run off leash, something I rarely do. As we started out, she always took off like a speeding bullet, running a couple of yards ahead of me. About three miles into our run I noticed that she began staying at my side and even running a few paces behind me until we finished.

Returning to our neighborhood course, I observed this same pattern. Willie was eager and bouncy during the first three miles of our run, then, as at the beach, she began to lose some zest. As this pattern recurred, I concluded that her daily limit was approximately three miles because up until that point she ran comfortably and easily.

As with all dogs, the time of year greatly affects Willie's capabilities. When it's cool outside, she seems to never get tired. Often after five or six miles she's still full of pep. Winter months tend to increase her comfortable limits to four or five miles. Although I'm uncertain of Willie's extreme limits, I believe I have a good understanding of how many miles a week she can comfortably handle. When I consider the fact that she needs only twenty minutes of running three times a week to stay aerobically fit, I realize there is no reason to overdo it.

Besides weather, there are other factors that will determine a dog's mileage limits. Age, breed, size, temperament, and exercise experience will affect how far a dog likes to run. The primary factor to observe, when attempting to determine your pet's running limitation, is the point at which he begins to tire, lag behind, or just plain lose interest.

Unlike people, dogs usually will stop when they are tired. However, loyalty and devotion may cause your pet to run more than normal if he were by himself. Only you are the best judge of your dog's limitations. If your dog never shows signs of wanting to stop, no matter how far or how long he's run, you should carefully watch for subtle changes of enthusiasm in him.

The question "How many miles is too many?" remains unanswered. However, as your dog's stamina and strength increase, he will undoubtedly enjoy accompanying you on longer runs and be able to run more often,

perhaps even daily. The object of conditioning your dog to run is not for you to brag about the number of miles covered, but to keep your pet physically fit, healthy, and happy.

STARTING UP — OWNERS

The same "3 x 20 Easy Plan" for starting dogs on a running program is also an excellent way for starting humans on a running program. This start-up plan (referenced on page 21) is especially safe for humans because it allows time to gradually build up the body by alternating walking and running until twenty minutes of continuous running is achieved. Beginners, older people, or those with health problems should only start this program after first receiving a complete physical examination.

Before starting to run, humans should also consider the desirability of warm-up exercises such as toe touches, arm circles, neck rolls, sit-ups, and leg stretches. Some runners prefer to stretch after they've been running awhile or after they've finished their run, which is also acceptable. In either case, it is important that the muscles are given an opportunity to flex and relax. A cool-down, either stretching or a five minute leisurely walk, is also a good way to end a run.

The ideal jogging pace for a beginner is one in which he can comfortably carry on a conversation. This is no problem for Richard Alderman and his dog, Stray, who, Richard says "is an interesting person to talk to." Joe Henderson has a harder time because his dog, Willie, "never asks him to make witty, intelligent conversation." However, the "talk test" (regardless of whom you choose to talk to) is the best way to make sure you are jogging at a comfortable and safe pace.

Inexperienced runners desiring more information on starting a running program can consult any number of available running books. Two particularly good books which are extremely easy to follow are: *The Runner's Handbook* by Bob Glover and Jack Shepherd, and *Jog, Run, Race* by Joe Henderson. There are also a vast number of health clubs, running clubs, and community organizations, such as local YMCAs and Park and Recreation Department centers, that offer jogging classes and can give advice to novice runners.

When jogging, "She's an interesting person to talk to," says Richard Alderman teasingly of his lively pet, Stray.

Once you've become a "regular" on the roads, running twenty minutes or more at least three times per week, your interest in running longer distances and/or more often will undoubtedly increase. You may even wish to challenge yourself occasionally by entering a "fun run." These organized events can be great fun because they are usually run over traffic-free courses in which frequent water stops are provided.

Fun runs typically range from three to six miles and often include a one- or two-mile race in addition to the main race. (Fun runs are generally advertised in the weekend section of local newspapers and in various running publications.) Since fun runs usually don't allow dogs, you'll have to pull through the race on your own, which should not be a problem if you've been following the "3 x 20 Easy Plan" for a number of months.

Just as with a dog's running program, when advancing, people should follow a "hard-easy" method of training. A mileage log, as previously suggested, is also useful when advancing because it helps prevent exceeding a ten percent mileage increase per week.

A side benefit of starting a jogging program at the same time as your dog is knowing you don't have to feel self-conscious about being a beginner. Most passersby have a tendency to concentrate on the dog rather than its owner.

OUTFITTING THE HUMAN

Running equipment is often taken for granted because, aside from clothes and shoes, little else is required. When discussing running apparel, almost anything is acceptable as long as it is comfortable and nonbinding. It's important to note, though, when running in cold weather, clothes are best worn in layers. Layering insulates the body more effectively, plus, layers can be removed in stages as the body heats up due to exertion.

Shoe selection, on the other hand, requires more consideration. Running shoes should fit comfortably, and be durable and well-cushioned to absorb the shock of the road. Shoes not specifically designed to absorb shock can cause lower leg and back pain.

What To Look For In A Running Shoe

It's wise to purchase running shoes from running specialty shops or sporting goods stores where you will find a wide variety of styles. Always try on shoes while wearing the type of socks you plan to run in and be sure the shoe you select meets the following minimum requirements:

Good Fit — The moment you try on a running shoe it should feel good. Generally, running shoes cannot be "broken in" to achieve a good fit. Allow a thumbnail width of space at the toe of the shoe, and make sure your toes have enough room to move and stretch out. It's common to wear a running shoe a half size larger than a regular dress shoe.

Black Outsole — The bottom of the shoe that contacts the ground should be made of a solid rubber, black tread outsole. Frequently referred to as a "carbon" outsole, this type of sole makes a shoe more abrasion-resistant.

Midsole Layer — There should be a good "in-between" layer of cushioning between the outsole and the inside of the shoe.

Appropriate Shoe Shape — Running shoes have two basic shapes, straight and curved, and how your feet strike the ground generally determines which shape is the right one for your foot.

Straight-shaped shoes, called "straight last" in the shoe industry, are characterized by a shoe bottom that appears neither flared inward nor outward at the forefoot of the shoe. Often with this type of shoe, it is difficult to distinguish the left shoe from the right shoe. Curved-shaped shoes, called "curve last" or "C-last" shoes in the industry, have a banana-shaped bottom and flare inward at the ball of the shoe.

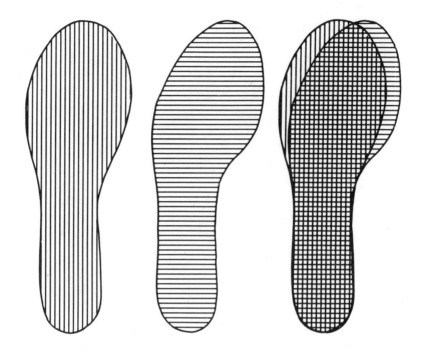

To determine the correct shape of shoe for your foot, turn your present running shoes or athletic shoes upside down and observe their heel area. If the heels roll inward, you are said to be an "over pronator," a condition usually caused by a collapsing of the arch, and a straight-shaped shoe is recommended. Straight-last shoes are also recommended for individuals of heavy weight. If the heels roll outward and the outside midsole layer is *obviously* compressed (not to be confused with outer heel wear, common with everyday use), you are called an "over supinator," and a curve-last shoe is recommended. Curved-shaped shoes are recommended in this case because they compensate by placing the toes slightly inward from the heel. Curve-last shoes are also recommended for individuals who run on the balls or toes of their feet.

If your shoes do not display either of the above signs of wear, you probably have average feet, and the general rule of thumb when choosing a running shoe is: Use a curve-last shoe if your arch is normal and a straight last shoe if you have flat feet. Moreover, if your present running shoes appear to be wearing evenly, they are probably the correct shoes for you, and there is little reason to change brands or styles.

Chapter 4

RUNNING ABILITY BY BREED

Knowledge of your dog's breed attributes and drawbacks is helpful when determining how much running he can safely handle. In this chapter we evaluate each breed's running capabilities, possible problems that might influence running potential, and what adjustments to make when jogging a show dog.

In the United States, dogs are divided into seven breed groups: Sporting, Hound, Working, Terriers, Toys, Non-Sporting, and Herding. Because classification in each breed group is mostly based on what a dog was originally bred to do, rather than how he actually evolved, it is presumed the more "running-related tasks" a dog's ancestors did, the better suited he'll be for jogging.

Dogs in the Sporting Group (frequently called the Gundog Group) were bred primarily to assist hunters by finding and retrieving game. The Hound Group contains dogs chiefly bred for tracking. The Working and Herding Groups contain dogs mainly bred for protecting livestock or people. Dogs in the Terrier Group (derived from the Latin word *"terra"* meaning earth) were bred to rout out vermin such as rats, badgers, and otters. *Toy* breeds were predominately bred for pleasure and companionship. These breeds are the smallest of all canines. The group which defies generalization is the Non-Sporting Group. It contains a variety of dog types with a wide range of characteristics and uses which do not fit into any of the other groups.

In general, long-legged dogs that are members of the Sporting, Hound, Working, and Herding groups are best suited for regular jogging. The Afghan Hound, Alaskan Malamute, Borzoi, Deerhound, Foxhound, Ibizan Hound, Irish Setter, Pharaoh Hound, Saluki, Siberian Husky, Vizsla, and Weimaraner are all breeds that possess exceptional running abilities and stamina. Working Foxhounds, for example, are tireless in the field and often run up to 100 miles a day. Alaskan Malamutes, too, can go all day, even while under the strain of pulling hundreds of pounds of weight on dog sleds.

This is not to say dogs in the other breed groups are not well suited for jogging. Airedales and Soft-Coated Wheaten Terriers, members of the Terrier Group, are two examples of breeds with lots of stamina and good jogging abilities. Likewise, the Dalmatian, a member of the Non-Sporting Group, can cover dozens of miles a day. These dogs commonly ran for

Ted Reed's two Great Danes, Chevas and Regal, are impressive running companions. But, as the chart in this chapter suggests, Danes should be at least eighteen months old before beginning a running program, and preferably not run over 25 miles per week.

miles alongside horse-drawn carriages during the eighteenth and mid-nineteenth centuries.

Incidentally, special mention should be made of the "track stars" of the canine world. These stars are the so-called sighthounds or coursing hounds. Characterized by a narrow, streamlined head, long, arched back, and a long tail which acts in the manner of a rudder, they include the Greyhound, Saluki, Borzoi, Whippet, and Afghan Hound. Greyhounds and Salukis are undoubtedly the fastest runners of all canines. Their long limbs, deep chest, and exceptionally well-developed heart and lungs allow them to reach speeds of forty miles per hour and more.

YOUR DOG'S POTENTIAL RUNNING ABILITY

To ascertain your particular breed's (or mixed-breed's) running potential, please refer to the third column of the Breed Profile Chart on page 34, entitled "Running Ability." In this column, each breed's potential running ability is rated. **Owners of mixed breeds should find the purebred breed their pet most closely resembles.**

Dogs with a "**Superior (S)**" rating make excellent running partners and can probably, with conditioning, run daily or run for long distances. However, for even these "super athletes," I suggest they not be run more than 25 to 35 miles per week. This equates to approximately 5 to 7 miles a day, five days a week.

After what was said earlier about a breed such as the Foxhound, 25 to 35 miles per week may seem conservative. Human marathoners, accustomed to running twice this amount, may also consider 25 to 35 miles per week conservative. Keep in mind, though, that as little as twenty minutes of exercise, three days a week is sufficient to maintain fitness in both dogs and humans.

Dogs with a "**Good (G)**" rating also make fine running partners, but may be less capable of running daily or for long distances. For dogs in this category, I advise no more than 18 to 25 miles per week. Running five days a week, this is equivalent to 4 or 5 miles a day.

Miss Whalen, an eager to run Labrador, is a breed of "Superior" running potential.

Dogs with a "**Fair (F)**" rating are least suited for jogging and should only run short distances. Fifteen miles per week is probably plenty for these dogs because, broken down, it can mean as much as three miles a day, five days a week.

One should not assume a dog with a "Superior" or "Good" rating can automatically run long-distances. Most of us would never consider running long distances without training and proper build up of our endurance. Similarly, even dogs capable of long-distance jogging need gradual conditioning in order to lengthen their distances and build up endurance. Again, all dogs should begin a running program using the "3 x 20 Easy Plan" described in the previous chapter.

Remember: These ratings are only guidelines. Consult your veterinarian for a final opinion on how much to run your dog.

"Sebastian (like Miss Whalen previously pictured) carries his leash around until he's taken for a run," says owner Susan Cabell of Boulder, Colorado.

JOGGING FOR SHOW DOGS

When preparing show dogs for movement in the ring, jogging can help a sloppily moving dog tighten up or enable the basically correct moving dog to develop a gait that is smooth, fully extended, and animated. Done incorrectly, however, jogging can actually cause a show dog more harm than good. Therefore, the most important factors show dog owners need to consider are: *not to run the dog too many miles or train on a surface or at a speed that could inhibit movement.*

Running a show dog too many miles could cause the dog's muscles to become over developed. A hard surface should be avoided as much as possible because it could cause bruised pads, injure a dog's shoulders, or break down his pasterns. Also, *never* run a show dog downhill, as this causes the dog to restrict his reach and can cause other movement problems. Running uphill, on the other hand, may cause you both to pant a little more, but it can benefit a show dog by strengthening a weak rear or developing rear drive.

The speed at which a show dog jogs can cause improper movement in the ring, too, so try to run at a speed that encourages the dog to move out freely, reaching and driving to full extension. Never allow a dog to run so slowly that he switches to a pace or moves in a choppy, restricted gate. (Dogs with correct angulation and, therefore, a longer stride will probably trot faster than ones with steeper angulation and a more restricted reach.)

A friend who breeds and shows Shelties experienced a movement problem not long ago with Rusty, a male Sheltie she regularly took jogging. Because they ran together on mostly well-traveled roads, the dog learned to stay close to his owner's left side. Later when Rusty was sent to a professional handler, the biggest problem was getting him to run ahead while in the ring. He wanted to stay too close to the handler's side — something that is not impressive in the show ring. It took almost a year before Rusty learned to run with animation and speed. Thus, encouraging a show dog to move with his head up, at the correct speed, and slightly ahead of the handler/owner (instead of in heel position) is of primary concern.

Starting a show dog on a running program is best accomplished using the "3 x 20 Easy Plan." This gradual, step-by-step approach should have the show dog in condition in no time. If the dog becomes stiff or lame at any time, however, discontinue or shorten workouts until he recovers. If run properly and mileage is kept to a minimum (not more than two miles per day is recommended), the dog's gait should be a pleasure to watch.

BREED PROFILE CHART

SIZE: S - small dogs to 28 lbs.   L - large dogs 45-75 lbs.
M - medium dogs 28-45 lbs.   G - giant dogs over 100 lbs.

AGE: Age dog can begin running (example: 8 mo., 1 yr.)

**RUNNING
ABILITY:** S - Superior   F - Fair
G - Good   P - Poor

**MAXIMUM
MILEAGE:** Recommended maximum miles dogs can run per week

**GROOMING
NEEDS:** R - Regular   F - Frequent
D - Daily   M - Minimal

Breed	Size	Age	Running Ability	Max. Mileage	Groom-ing	General Comments (and Breed Group Classification)
Affenpinscher	S	8 mos	F	15	R	TOY - Originally bred in Germany as ratting dog.
Afghan Hound	L	1 yr	S	35	D	HOUND - Originally used to hunt wolves and gazelle. Very strong animal capable of great speed.
Airedale	L	1 yr	S	35	R	TERRIER - Ancestors used for rodent control. Largest of terrier group. Lots of stamina.
Akita	L	1 yr	G	25	R	WORKING - Was bred to hunt wild boar in Japan. Swift dog, good swimmer.
Alaskan Malamute	L	1 yr	S	35	R	WORKING - Largest of sleddogs. Energetic and powerful. Likes cold climate.
American Eskimo	S	8 mos	G	25	R	Not AKC recognized. Has strong hunting instincts.
American Staffordshire Terrier	M	1 yr	G	25	M	TERRIER - Also known as Pit Bull Terrier. Good rat catcher. Keep leashed as these dogs cannot resist fights with other dogs.
American Water Spaniel	M	8 mos	S	35	F	SPORTING - Working gun dog. Strong swimmer and excellent retriever.
Australian Shepherd	M	1 yr	S	35	R	One of the most popular breeds not recognized by AKC. Working dog with stamina, strength, and agility.
Australian Terrier	S	8 mos	G	25	R	TERRIER - Speedy rodent catcher. Alert and active dog. One of the smallest working terriers.
Basenji	S	8 mos	S	35	M	HOUND - Barkless dog used for hunting. Fast and tireless. Playful, catlike, clean dogs.

Breed	Size	Age	Running Ability	Max. Mileage	Grooming	General Comments (and Breed Group Classification)
Basset Hound	M	1 yr	F	15	M	HOUND - Originally used for hunting deer and rabbits. Extraordinary scenting powers. Choose a pup with straight limbs.
Beagle	S	8 mos	G	25	M	HOUND - Hunted in packs for rabbits. Also good gun dog. Healthy breed.
Bearded Collie	M	1 yr	S	35	R	HERDING - Good sheep and cattle herding capabilities. Healthy, enthusiastic, energetic dog needing plenty of exercise.
Bedlington Terrier	S	8 mos	G	25	F	TERRIER - May have been crossed with a whippet or greyhound originally. Capable of great speed and is quite graceful.
Belgian Sheepdog, Tervuren, Malinois	L	1 yr	S	35	M	HERDING - Good obedience workers or herding dogs. Hardy.
Bernese Mountain Dog	L	1 yr	G	25	M	WORKING - Draft breed originating in Switzerland. Hardy. Thrives in cold climate.
Bichon Frise	S	8 mos	F	15	F	NON-SPORTING - French origin. Gentle disposition. Poodle-like coat.
Black & Tan Coonhound	L	1 yr	S	35	M	HOUND - Used to hunt raccoon and possum. Hard working, fast, strong, and sturdy.
Bloodhound	L	1 yr	S	35	M	HOUND - Keen sense of smell, excellent tracking dog.
Border Collie	L	1 yr	S	35	R	MISCELLANEOUS - Sheep and cattle herder. Healthy, with speed and stamina. Needs lots of exercise.
Border Terrier	S	8 mos	G	25	R	TERRIER - Bred to hunt fox. Active and hardy with wiry, double coat.
Borzoi	L	1 yr	S	35	F	HOUND - Coursing dog of beauty and grace, with great power and speed.
Boston Terrier	S	8 mos	F	15	M	NON-SPORTING - Native American breed. Great companion and housepet. Bulldog-type muzzle.
Bouvier Des Flandres	L	1½ yrs	S	35	R	HERDING - Herding or guard dog. Big boned, muscular dog, needs strong discipline.
Boxer	L	1½ yrs	S	35	M	WORKING - Cousin to most bulldog types. Intelligent, with courage and stamina.
Briard	L	1 yr	S	35	R	HERDING - Herding or guard dog. Strong, well-mannered breed of French origin.

Breed	Size	Age	Running Ability	Max. Mileage	Grooming	General Comments (and Breed Group Classification)
Brittany Spaniel	S	8 mos	S	35	R	SPORTING - Only AKC recognized Spaniel that points. Capable gun dog, agile, tireless.
Brussels Griffon	S	8 mos	F	15	R	TOY - Originally bred to catch vermin. Intelligent but sensitive and sometimes stubborn.
Bulldog	M	8 mos	P	15	R	NON-SPORTING - Build does not permit fast running. Can't tolerate heat.
Bullmastiff	L	1 yr	G	25	M	WORKING - Massive guard dog. Needs firm handling.
Bull Terrier	M	8 mos	S	25	M	TERRIER - Fighting dogs. Hardy, active, agile. Not recommended for children.
Cairn Terrier	S	8 mos	G	25	M	TERRIER - Energetic, hardy, likes to dig.
Cavalier King Charles Spaniel	S	8 mos	F	15	R	MISCELLANEOUS - Small, hardy lap dog.
Chesapeake Bay Retriever	L	1 yr	S	35	M	SPORTING - Excellent swimmer and retriever.
Chihuahau	S	8 mos	F	15	M	TOY - More robust than it looks. Short and long-coated varieties.
Chow Chow	L	1 yr	G	25	F	NON-SPORTING - Powerful, compact, active breed.
Clumber Spaniel	L	1 yr	G	25	R	SPORTING - Heaviest of all Spaniels. Excellent retriever.
Cocker Spaniel	S	8 mos	G	25	F	SPORTING - Great companion dog. Originally bred for hunting and retrieving.
Collie	L	1 yr	S	35	R	HERDING - Hardy, intelligent, easily trained. Smooth and rough coated varieties.
Curley-Coated Retriever	L	1 yr	S	35	M	SPORTING - Excellent swimmer and retriever. Hardy, affectionate, easy to train.
Dachshund	S	8-10 mos	F	15	M	HOUND - Despite short legs, these dogs like exercise, are hardy, alert, and responsive.
Dalmatian	L	1 yr	S	35	M	NON-SPORTING - Agile, muscular dog with speed and stamina. Sensible, well-mannered.
Dandie Dinmont Terrier	S	8 mos	F	15	R	TERRIER - Excellent watchdog, very active, intelligent, but with a mind of their own.
Doberman Pincher	L	1 yr	S	35	M	WORKING - Powerful, agile guardian. Intelligent, easily trained, need discipline.
English Cocker Spaniel	M	8 mos	G	25	R	SPORTING - Active sporting and gun dog. Merry disposition, excellent companion.

Breed	Size	Age	Running Ability	Max. Mileage	Grooming	General Comments (and Breed Group Classification)
English Setter	L	1 yr	S	35	F	SPORTING - Gundog that uses scent and sight to locate game.
English Shepherd	L	1 yr	S	35	R	Not AKC recognized - Good herding and working dog.
English Springer Spaniel	L	1 yr	S	35	R	SPORTING - Pheasant hunter and good retriever. Strong, active breed.
English Toy Spaniel	S	8 mos	F	15	R	TOY - Ancient Eastern breed. Hardy for its size.
Field Spaniel	M	8 mos	S	35	R	SPORTING - One of the lesser-known sporting dogs. Sound, with endurance and moderate speed.
Flat-Coated Retriever	L	1 yr	S	35	R	SPORTING - Good swimmer, with drive and perseverance, delightful temperament.
Fox Terrier	S	8 mos	G	25	R	TERRIER - Smooth and wire-haired varieties. Energetic, active.
Foxhound (American & English)	L	1 yr	S	35	R	HOUND - Likes vigorous exercise. Great stamina, enthusiasm.
German Shepherd	L	1 yr	S	35	M	HERDING - Loyal, courageous, able to retain training for special services. Hardy, intelligent.
German Short-haired and Wirehaired Pointer	L	1 yr	S	35	R	SPORTING - All-purpose hunting dog. Sturdy and energetic.
Giant Schnauzer	G	1½ yrs	S	35	F	WORKING - Likes vigorous exercise. Robust, loyal, watchful.
Golden Retriever	L	1 yr	S	35	R	SPORTING - Ideal family pet or gun dog. Needs plenty of exercise.
Gordon Setter	L	1 yr	S	35	R	SPORTING - Good bird dog or companion. Needs lots of exercise.
Great Dane	G	1½ yrs	G	25	M	WORKING - A dog of dignity, strength, and courage, with a powerful body.
Great Pyrenees	L	1 yr	G	25	R	WORKING - Ancient breed bred to guard flocks in harsh climate.
Greyhound	L	1 yr	S	35	M	HOUND - Coursing hound capable of great speed. Must be controlled while jogging. Excellent companion dog.
Harrier	L	1 yr	S	35	M	HOUND - Smaller version of the Foxhound, and somewhat slower. Needs exercise.
Ibizan Hound	L	1 yr	S	35	M	HOUND - Agile, strong coursing dog. Healthy, lively companion.
Irish Setter	L	1 yr	S	35	R	SPORTING - Active, bold, lovable, loyal. Slow developing, but an excellent gun dog.

Breed	Size	Age	Running Ability	Max. Mileage	Groom-ing	General Comments (and Breed Group Classification)
Irish Terrier	S	8 mos	G	25	R	TERRIER - Hardy, adaptable; hunts small game and will also retrieve; makes a good guard dog.
Irish Water Spaniel	L	1 yr	S	35	F	SPORTING - Tallest spaniel, loves water; good retriever and strong swimmer.
Irish Wolfhound	G	1½ yrs	S	35	R	HOUND - Ancient breed used originally for hunting wolves. Needs space and plenty of exercise.
Italian Greyhound	S	8 mos	G	25	M	TOY - Smallest gazehound. Likes exercise, is hardy, yet prefers being a lap dog.
Jack Russell Terrier	S	8 mos	G	25	R	Not AKC recognized.
Japanese Chin	S	8 mos	F	15	F	TOY - Small Oriental breed. Hardy, alert companion.
Keeshond	M	8 mos	G	25	R	NON-SPORTING - Hardy, Arctic breed with luxurious coat. Companion and watchdog.
Kerry Blue Terrier	S	8 mos	G	25	F	TERRIER - Working or retrieving breed. Long-lived, active, adaptable.
Komondor	L	1 yr	G	25	R	WORKING - Protector of flocks; a dog of courage, strength, and self-reliance.
Kuvasz	L	1 yr	S	35	R	WORKING - Used for herding, guarding, or hunting big game. Sensitive, devoted, untiring.
Labrador Retriever	L	1 yr	S	35	M	SPORTING - Retriever, often also used for search and rescue or as guide dogs. Active, easy-going temperament.
Lakeland Terrier	S	8 mos	S	35	F	TERRIER - Bold, gay, friendly, and energetic dog. Originally bred to hunt foxes.
Lhasa Apso	S	8 mos	F	15	F	NON-SPORTING - Hardy, gay, active, and watchful housepet.
Maltese	S	8 mos	F	15	F	TOY - Healthy dog, likes exercise despite small size.
Manchester Terrier	S	8 mos	G	25	M	TERRIER - Rodent-killing terrier with coursing breeds in its background. Intelligent, lively.
Mastiff	G	1½ yrs	G	25	M	WORKING - Powerful dog originally bred for fighting. Likes having a job to do.
Miniature Pinscher	S	8 mos	F	15	M	TOY - Small version of Doberman. Active, lively.
Miniature Poodle	S	8 mos	F	15	F	NON-SPORTING - Active, intelli-gent, elegant, and hardier than it seems. Likes water.

Breed	Size	Age	Running Ability	Max. Mileage	Grooming	General Comments (and Breed Group Classification)
Miniature Schnauzer	S	8 mos	G	25	F	TERRIER - Robust, active dog fond of children. Healthy.
Newfoundland	G	1½ yrs	S	35	R	WORKING - Bred for rescue work. Good swimmer, strong and robust. Capable of draft work, good companion.
Norfolk Terrier	S	8 mos	G	25	M	TERRIER - Short-legged, small, sturdy, alert, and fearless.
Norwich Terrier	S	8 mos	G	25	M	TERRIER - Hardy, happy-go-lucky, tolerant of any weather.
Norweigan Elkhound	L	1 yr	S	35	R	HOUND - Used to hunt and hold elk. Energetic, need firm but gentle handling.
Old English Sheepdog	L	1 yr	S	35	F	HERDING - Loveable, agile, affectionate, with a bear-like, shuffling gait.
Otter Hound	L	1 yr	S	35	R	HOUND - Excellent swimmer and retriever. Likes exercise. Hardy and devoted.
Papillon	S	8 mos	F	15	F	TOY - Also called "Butterfly dog" because of its ears. Although dainty, they are quite hardy.
Pekingese	S	8 mos	P	15	F	TOY - Dignified but stubborn. Short muzzle may cause breathing difficulties during vigorous exercise.
Pharaoh Hound	L	1 yr	S	35	M	HOUND - Swift, powerful, elegant, and hardy. One of the oldest domestic breeds.
Pointer	L	1 yr	S	35	M	SPORTING - Enjoys field work.
Pomeranian	S	8 mos	F	15	F	TOY - Lively lap dog, sturdy for his diminutive size.
Portuguese Water Dog	L	1 yr	G	25	F	WORKING - Calm, intelligent, rugged breed with non-allergenic, waterproof coat, and webbed feet.
Pug	S	8 mos	P	15	M	TOY - Avoid vigorous exertion, loveable, staunch companion.
Puli	M	8 mos	S	35	R	HERDING - Vigorous, active dog with long, corded coat. Used for guarding or driving sheep.
Redbone Coonhound	L	1 yr	S	35	M	Not AKC recognized. Strong, muscular, active dog, excellent hunter.
Rhodesian Ridgeback	L	1 yr	S	35	M	HOUND - Strong, muscular, and active, capable of endurance and speed.
Rottweiler	L	1 yr	S	35	M	WORKING - Old Roman drover breed, often used for guardian or police work.
St. Bernard	G	1½ yrs	G	25	R	WORKING - Bred for rescue work in Switzerland. Slow maturing yet relatively short-lived. Don't over-work as puppies.

Breed	Size	Age	Running Ability	Max. Mileage	Groom-ing	General Comments (and Breed Group Classification)
Saluki	L	1 yr	S	35	R	HOUND - Swift, graceful coursing breed.
Samoyed	M	8 mos	S	35	R	WORKING - Sturdy white dog with a muscular body and legs built for speed. Used as sled dogs and guardians.
Schipperke	S	8 mos	G	25	M	NON-SPORTING - Hardy, active little dogs. Jovial companions.
Scottish Deerhound	L	1½ yrs	S	35	R	HOUND - A deer hunting hound of great size, speed, and agility.
Scottish Terrier	S	8 mos	G	25	F	TERRIER - Short legged, strong, active dog with typical terrier personality.
Sealyham Terrier	S	8 mos	G	25	R	HERDING - Active, intelligent, hardy, small breed with working dog temperament. Easily trained.
Shar-Pei	M	8 mos	G	25	R	Not AKC recognized. Unusual breed with wrinkled skin and naturally blue-black tongue.
Shetland Sheepdog	S	8 mos	G	25	R	HERDING - Active, intelligent, hardy, small breed with working dog temperament. Easily trained.
Shih Tzu	S	8 mos	F	15	F	TOY - Very active, lively, and alert. Primarily a house pet.
Siberian Husky	M	8 mos	S	35	R	WORKING - Great physical endurance and speed. Widely used in dog sled racing.
Silky Terrier	S	8 mos	G	25	F	TOY - Despite size Silkies have well-developed terrier instincts and can be very active.
Skye Terrier	S	8 mos	G	25	F	TERRIER - Tireless dog bred to hunt fox, otter, and badger.
Soft-Coated Wheaten Terrier	M	8 mos	S	35	R	TERRIER - Used on farms in its native Ireland. Hardy, strong, active breed.
Staffordshire Bull Terrier	M	1 yr	G	25	R	TERRIER - May find it hard to resist fighting other dogs.
Standard Poodle	L	1 yr	G	25	F	NON-SPORTING - Robust and healthy dogs with lots of stamina despite its pampered image. Enjoys water.
Standard Schnauzer	M	8 mos	S	35	F	WORKING - Good watchdog, originally bred to catch rodents and drive cattle.
Sussex Spaniel	M	8 mos	S	35	F	SPORTING - Tireless, strong dog, but not widely known.
Tibetan Spaniel	S	8 mos	G	25	F	NON-SPORTING. Cat-like personality, affectionate, smart.
Tibetan Terrier	S	8 mos	G	25	R	NON-SPORTING - Not really a terrier because these dogs were mainly used for farm work.
Toy Fox Terrier	S	8 mos	G	25	M	Not AKC recognized. Hardy and healthy dog with spirit.

Breed	Size	Age	Running Ability	Max. Mileage	Groom-ing	General Comments (and Breed Group Classification)
Toy Manchester Terrier	S	8 mos	G	25	M	TOY - Good rat catcher. Lively dog with sleek, clean build.
Toy Poodle	S	8 mos	F	15	F	TOY - Replica of Miniature and Standard Poodle.
Vizsla	L	1 yr	S	35	M	SPORTING - Points instinctively, has keen sense of smell and good retrieving abilities.
Weimaraner	L	1 yr	S	35	M	SPORTING - Originally used on big game. Muscular animal. Happiest when given a job to do.
Welsh Corgi Cardigan & Pembroke	S	8 mos	G	25	R	HERDING - Hardy and tireless; alert, agreeable house pets or able herders.
Welsh Springer Spaniel	M	8 mos	S	35	R	SPORTING - Good gun dog and water dog with strong, muscular body. Hardy and tireless dog.
Welsh Terrier	S	8 mos	S	35	F	TERRIER - Robust, hardy dog that can be easily trained to hunt and work with a gun.
West Highland White Terrier	S	8 mos	G	25	F	TERRIER - Used as working terrier, enjoys energetic activity.
Whippet	S	8 mos	S	35	M	HOUND - Capable of running 35-40 miles per hour. Hardy dog but should sleep indoors.
Wirehaired Pointing Griffon	M	8 mos	S	35	R	SPORTING - Pointer, works well in water, likes vigorous exercise.
Yorkshire Terrier	S	8 mos	F	15	F	TOY - Boundless energy for its size. Tiny, but spirited, with a Terrier's temperament.

Chapter 5

TIPS FOR SAFE RUNNING

Helpful hints on any subject tend to point out the obvious, common sense stuff we already know. However, usually when I take the time to review someone's tips, I find one or two points I can put to good use. So, whether you decide to run with your dog on country roads or busy city streets, these tips will make your runs safer and more enjoyable.

• *Always have your dog on a leash when you run with him.* With a leash you can control his gait and his steps more effectively. A quality leather or cotton web, six-foot leash is best for running. There is a wide variety of collar styles to choose from; optimally, a training, or choke, collar of steel or nylon is preferable. A training collar should have pounded, flat links and fit snugly so that clean, corrective jerks will be quickly released. Most trainers feel that spiked choke collars are inhumane and unnecessary. A pet identification tag stating the owner's name, address, and phone number, plus a rabies vaccination or pet registration tag are a must for your dog's collar. I always tell my dog, "This way you'll be able to identify me should anything happen."

• *When forced to run on streets, face the traffic with your dog in the heel position on your left side.* Some dog joggers say they prefer having their dog on their right side, away from the curb, to prevent them from sniffing everything. It's really safer, however, to keep your dog on your left side, so he's less likely to interfere with traffic flow. Also, using the heel position is in keeping with obedience training procedures which depend on consistency.

Either a collar or harness is acceptable for controlling dogs while jogging. Dick Reeves prefers a harness to which Morgan, his Wirehaired Fox Terrier, has no objection.

• *Before crossing busy intersections, stop, tell your dog to sit, then proceed when clear.*

• *Bring your dog closer in to you when passing or approaching other people, dogs, bicycles, etc.*

• *Be consistent with your commands and use lots of praise.* When your dog pulls ahead on the lead, try adding the word "back" to his vocabulary. Give a quick backward jerk along with the command, and pull him back into position.

• *Because of traffic considerations it is better to run in the early morning or evening.*

• *Put a reflective collar on your dog and wear light-colored clothing and/or reflective gear when running after dark.*

• *Before starting out, possibly while you're stretching, let your dog urinate and/or defecate.* Invariably, five minutes into the run dogs start pulling on their leads, wanting "to go." Be discreet and remember to have respect for other people's property. Better yet, carry a couple of small plastic storage bags to use for cleaning up.

New Yorker Elizabeth Kallen believes in giving dog owners a good image. She always carries a few plastic bags just in case her dog, Buster, must relieve himself in an inappropriate spot.

• *Running on hard surfaces, such as concrete, will usually keep a dog's nails worn down.* Nevertheless, check your dog's nails regularly, including the dewclaw, because long nails can grow into the footpad or cause him to stand improperly. They also cause the pads to splay apart, thus providing less support and flexibility.

• *Many school running tracks do not allow dogs, so respect their rules.* If dogs are allowed, run in the outermost lanes. By the way, don't let your dog relieve himself in areas that students will be likely to use.

• *Enter a fun run only if you have the approval of the race director.* Even then, remember that other participants run the risk of being tripped by the leash or having to make a major effort to go around you and your dog.

• *Run your dog off-leash only in non-congested areas and watch him closely for signs of fatigue.* While you're running one mile, your dog may zig-zag around and log many more.

• *Smooth, free-from-traffic roads and paths make excellent running trails.* Running surfaces such as smooth dirt roads, grass, or wet beachfront are best, followed by gravel or macadam. Concrete and blacktop should be avoided whenever possible, especially during summer months when these surfaces can get extremely hot and burn a dog's footpads. Be cautious when changing surfaces. Your dog's pads may be conditioned to one particular type of surface but not to others. Unfortunately, I found this out at my dog's expense.

I usually run with Willie on dirt/woodchip paths, paved hike and bike trails, or neighborhood streets. A few summers ago, the city of Houston decided to upgrade one of their hike and bike trails and repave the old surface with blacktop. Soon afterward, we were out running on a hot day. I was being very careful and made sure that Willie got plenty of water, stopping at a fountain or pond every twenty minutes so she could cool off. I remember being proud of my extra regard due to the heat.

An important factor I overlooked was the change in the running surface. The day following our run Willie was lethargic and didn't want to move around. I couldn't figure out what was wrong with her. Two days later I noticed that her pads were beginning to peel, and I knew. This proves how sensitive a dog's footpads can be to different surfaces, especially fresh blacktop.

Note: Some veterinarians recommend trying this mixture for toughening up dogs' feet:

        30 milligrams (1 ounce) Tincture Benzoin
        1 ounce Alum
        2 ounces Tannic Acid
        8 ounces Petroleum Jelly
        1/3 ounce Balsam of Peru

Mix ingredients together thoroughly and apply to pads. (Ingredients are available in most drugstores.) Commercial products are also available.

ENVIRONMENTAL FACTORS

There are times when the environment can spoil well-intended plans for a jog with pets. However, with a little respect for Mother Nature and the following advice, you should be able to run with your dog year-round. Since dogs do not tolerate hot weather as well as humans, two of the most important environmental factors to bear in mind are heat and humidity. Consider Howard Kunz and his five-year-old English Setter, Duke, who once suffered a bad case of heatstroke.

Heat and Humidity

Running Duke in cold weather or snow "would be a picnic," says Howard. On the other hand, because of his dog's close encounter with heatstroke, Howard is extremely cautious when running Duke in hot weather. While running on a recent summer day Duke "just pulled over and laid down," recalls his owner. Howard sprayed water on the dog and waited about twenty minutes before walking him home. Soon thereafter, he took him to a veterinarian. Howard considered submerging Duke in the nearby bayou, but didn't do so because he questioned the water's hygienic conditions (a reasonable reservation considering our present pollution conditions). What scared Howard the most was the fact that he didn't really know what to do.

Knowledge of hot weather problems such as heat exhaustion and heatstroke is very important. Heat exhaustion results from a loss of fluids (dehydration). Heatstroke (or heat prostration) results when one's body temperature becomes too high and, in effect, overheats. When dogs suffer from heatstroke, the physiological mechanisms ordinarily used to regulate their body temperature, such as panting, prove insufficient.

Detecting Heatstroke

The signs of heatstroke include an extremely high temperature (105° F. to 110° F.); uncontrollable panting; a fast, pounding pulse; blue tongue and gums (except in Chows and Shar Peis); frothing (thick white bubbles) at the mouth; and loss of consciousness. To treat heatstroke, the high body temperature must be lowered rapidly to avoid brain damage or death. Hose or bathe your dog in cold water and apply ice packs to the head and between the thighs until the temperature drops below 102° F. (Canine body temperature is measured by using a rectal thermometer.) Since body fluids must be replaced, small amounts of water or crushed ice cubes should be given. To make sure that your dog is all right, see your veterinarian as soon as possible.

As it turned out, Howard Kunz handled his dog's heatstroke situation better than he thought. Incidentally, his veterinarian has since assured him of the water's sanitation, and Howard now lets Duke cool off whenever he wants. They have never had another close call with heatstroke.

Owners of smaller breeds with short noses (such as Boxers, Bulldogs, and Pekingese), old and/or overweight dogs should remember that these pets are less able to regulate body temperature in hot weather. This makes them especially prone to heatstroke.

Ed Hall runs five to seven days a week with his Whippet named Whippet. A conscientious owner, Ed allows his pet to cool off whenever she's ready. Sometimes, however, his actions are misinterpreted and he hears complaints from strangers who think Whippet is sweating due to overexertion. Of course, these individuals didn't see Whippet minutes before when she dunked herself in a puddle along the trail. Panting is the primary way dogs sweat, and they dissipate about sixty to seventy percent of their body heat through this method. (The remainder is dispelled through the skin.) Hence, excessive panting is a better indication than sweating that a dog is being overworked.

Ed Hall's Whippet, named Whippet, is a tireless running companion, averaging 30 miles per week year-round. During warm weather both dog and owner make frequent water stops.

Humidity alone does not cause problems; only when it's combined with heat does it become a medical hazard. As humidity increases, tolerance to heat decreases. This can be seen in the straight line relationship depicted in the Heat Tolerance Graph below. This critical line runs from 100° F. with thirty percent humidity to 85° F. with ninety-five percent humidity. Every five-degree rise in temperature requires a twenty percent decrease in humidity to offset the combined effect of heat and humidity on dogs.

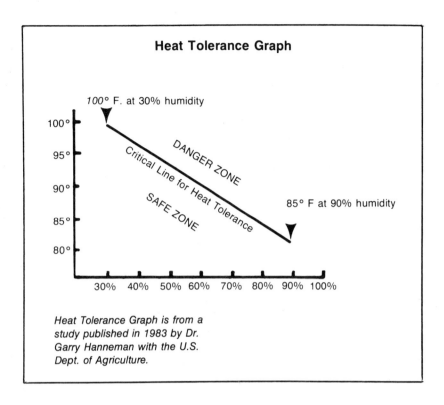

Heat Tolerance Graph

100° F. at 30% humidity

85° F at 90% humidity

DANGER ZONE

Critical Line for Heat Tolerance

SAFE ZONE

Heat Tolerance Graph is from a study published in 1983 by Dr. Garry Hanneman with the U.S. Dept. of Agriculture.

Tips For Hot Weather Running

- Run during the coolest times of the day.
- When exercising in hot weather, humans should try to drink fluids every twenty minutes. Dogs also should be given small amounts of water at least every twenty minutes. After running, and once your dog has completely cooled down and stopped panting, give water freely. Before this time give water only in small amounts.
- Use more caution when running dark-colored dogs. They absorb more heat than light-colored dogs.
- Short haircuts for long-haired dogs won't necessarily keep them cooler. Remember: A dog's fur helps insulate him from heat and protects him from sunburn.
- Keep a careful eye on your dog's breathing and general condition. Let him rest more often if he pants excessively or lags behind.
- If mosquitoes or other insects are abundant, consider using an insect repellent on your dog.

- Let your dog lie down in puddles or jump in (snake-free) ponds, creeks, etc., whenever he wants to. Splash water on his head to keep the brain cool.

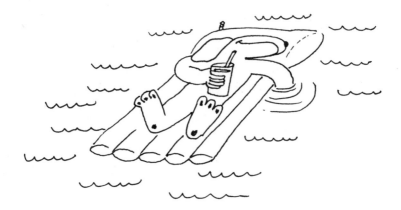

- When high humidity causes your dog's breathing to become labored, keep him at home.

Cold Weather And Snow

A dog's coat generally offers protection against extreme cold. Therefore, it's best not to clip a dog's hair during winter months. Avoid baths, too, unless absolutely necessary. Dogs run a good chance of catching a cold any time they get wet. To maintain a thick and healthy coat throughout the winter, increase your pet's supply of food, particularly protein. Talk to your veterinarian about adding vitamins and oil supplements to your dog's diet.

Owners of short-haired dogs might consider buying their pet a sweater for really cold days. While you might think sweaters are standard attire for little gray Poodles owned by little old ladies or that they will turn your "Brutus" into a sissy, think again. Sweaters make good sense, particularly if your dog shivers in the cold. Buy one that fits snugly around the dog's body, especially his stomach. Or, make a "poor-man's sweater," like Conrad McCarthy, a native Californian, does for his Weimaraner, Poleta Desert Wind.

According to Conrad, "An adequate dog sweatshirt can be fashioned from an old fun-run T-shirt and about four safety pins [from fun-run race numbers]." Moreover, if you've run in as many fun-runs as Conrad, your dog will have a selection of "sweaters" to last him weeks.

During chilling weather Conrad McCarthy occasionally loans his Weimaraner, Poleta Desert Wind, an old T-shirt.

Frostbite is rare in dogs, but prolonged exposure to severe cold could affect areas less insulated by hair, such as the ears, tail, scrotum, and paws. Massaging frozen areas could cause permanent damage, so the best way to restore body temperature is to immerse the animal in a tub of warm (102° F. to 105° F.) water or cover with an electric blanket. After thawing the frozen areas, keep them dry and lubricated with an antiseptic ointment or cream. If your dog has discomfort or pain, or if the skin seems to be infected, see a veterinarian.

Wind-chill factors (cold temperatures combined with wind) also pose health problems. When the wind-chill temperature is extremely low, keep your dog's trips outside to a minimum. Remember, when you're first starting out on cold days, run into the wind and return home with the wind at your back.

According to the American Society for the Prevention of Cruelty to Animals, "More dogs are lost during the winter than during any other season." Therefore, don't let your dog run off leash in snow. Dogs frequently lose their scent in snow and ice and can easily become lost. They may also panic during a snowstorm and run away. Be cautious of icy, slushy areas that are slippery. They can cause "ice balls" to form between the digits of a dog's foot. Salt and other chemicals used to melt snow on streets and sidewalks are irritants to a dog's feet. These substances are especially harmful when swallowed, so thoroughly wipe off your dog's legs, stomach, and feet when you get home.

51

Never leave a dog alone in a car during cold weather. Cars act as refrigerators in the winter, holding in the cold, and can cause dogs to literally freeze to death. Also, *beware of antifreeze.* Because of its sweet taste, animals are attracted to it. *As little as two tablespoons are enough to kill a 15-pound animal, so be sure to clean up spills thoroughly.*

Pollution, Poisons, and Pollens

It has been reported that dogs suffer from exhaust pollution more than people because they are closer to the ground where pollutants tend to be more concentrated. Conclusive or not, the worst place to run with your dog is along a highway or busy, city street. It is also believed that carbon monoxide and other pollutants from cars dissipate quickly only beyond 50 feet, another reason to keep your distance from major roadways.

Insecticides, herbicides, ant poison, pool chemicals, and poisoned bait for rodents are all harmful to pets. Additionally, the components in these substances tend to change regularly, thus occasionally leaving veterinarians at a loss for finding an appropriate antidote. Avoid perfect, weedless lawns where insecticides may be abundant and could be absorbed through your dog's footpads.

Pollens can also irritate your pet's respiratory system. When dirty air passes through a dog's breathing tubes, it is cleaned of dust particles, bacteria, and viruses by microscopic hairs and mucus. Occasionally, dogs will cough up this mucus. It is a yellowish, watery liquid that is simply part of their general "housecleaning" system.

If your dog continually bites and scratches, licks his paws, rubs his face, or has a generalized redness of skin, check with a veterinarian to see if he has an allergy. Often antihistamines can help relieve these symptoms just as they can for humans.

Fog

It is much more difficult for motorists to see during foggy conditions, so run on well-lit, familiar roads without much traffic. Wear red or orange clothes, since they provide the most contrast in fog, and run facing the traffic.

Other Dogs

There is nothing more annoying than being chased by a dog. In most cities, dogs are forbidden to roam at large. When off their owner's property they are required by law to either be leashed or under their owner's direct control. Nevertheless, if you run down any neighborhood street you'll undoubtedly be followed by a dog, with no owner in sight. Therefore, it is useful to know something about a dog's nature and body language in case one of these menaces appear.

Why do dogs like to chase people or things? Wolflike tendencies such as hunting, tracking, biting, and prey-killing are instinctive traits present in all dogs, and any moving object may trigger a dog's prey-chasing instincts. In other words, these objects have become "prey substitutes."

Most dogs guard their home turf and willingly retreat to their boundary limits.

Crossing to the opposite side of the street may be enough to avoid a dog's territory. Should a dog run at you, one of the most important things to remember is to stay calm. The threatening dog, as well as your own, can easily pick up on your emotions, and fear tends to encourage aggression in dogs. Always maintain your footing. A trip or fall can give a belligerent dog control.

The following body language will help you better anticipate a dog's intentions.

Friendly or Submissive Signals

- Avoids eye contact ; looks to the side

- Exposes throat ; grins

- Tucks tail between hind legs and wags, or holds tail high, flagging to and fro while ears are flat and body is low

- Lowers head beneath height of his tail, crouches, pounces or thrusts about in an effort to be playful

- Backs up or runs to the side, inviting your dog to chase him

Aggressive Signals

- Stares directly at you or your dog

- Curls lips open to show canine teeth and snarls or emits a low growl

- Raises ears forward

- Hair raised on shoulders and rump and hackles raised

- Neck arches and head is raised. Be especially wary if this position changes to lowered head with neck extended and he points in your direction

- Stiff legged; raises a front paw

- Slow-wagging, high-arched tail

Methods to discourage a stray dog

1. Give an authoritative "No" or "Go home."

2. Stay calm. If you scream or wave your hands and arms around, it may provoke him.

3. Bluff. Pretend to pick up a rock and throw it.

4. Stop and make friends. Talk to him in a soft but firm voice.

5. Throw a stone near him and back off slowly, always facing him.

6. Visit his owner.

7. If the problem persists, call the Animal Control Center in the vicinity.

Dog Bites—What To Do

Should you or your dog get bitten by another dog, stay calm and don't shout; this may only provoke another bite. Should the dog attempt to bite again, try placing something, such as a jacket or T-shirt between you and the dog's mouth.

Whether or not rabies is suspected, immediately report your bite to the city or county health department. In addition, immediately contact your doctor (or veterinarian if your dog has been bitten) within twelve hours.

Chapter 6

GETTING THERE AND BACK: WHAT TO DO IN THE CAR AND ON THE STREET

Running with your dog in the country, when on vacation or in different areas of your neighborhood, can make jogging more exciting. But in order to explore new running places, you'll probably, at one time or another, have to hop in your car to get there. Thus, it is helpful to have a pet who is at ease during car rides.

I never gave this subject much thought because my dog absolutely adores car rides. The words "Willie, go?" are her favorites, and car rides almost outrank the other main pleasures in her life: dog treats, chasing cats, and the mailman. But not too long ago, an acquaintance told me of his dog's fear of cars. The thought of driving his dog to a park to run seemed out of the question, considering past experiences. Since then I've discovered that this apprehension is not uncommon. This chapter explains how to teach your dog to ride in the car, offers information about car carriers for owners who think they might prefer this form of transportation, and suggests ten ways to help turn your pet's car rides into joy rides. In addition, the last part of the chapter discusses the problem of what to do should your dog get lost.

For the moment, Kevin Kelleher allows running buddy, Sheik, to demonstrate how not to transport pets. Sheik normally enjoys a safe ride in the back seat, tied securely for protection.

RIDER EDUCATION

Teaching pets to ride in a car is usually easier if you start training while they are very young. Older dogs may take longer to train, especially if their car trips have been limited to visits to the veterinarian's office. They need to be made to understand that all trips don't end with a shot.

For young and old dogs alike, start out with a short ride, say ten minutes or less, every day for a week. A couple of trips around the block will suffice. During the second week, gradually start increasing travel time until your pet is able to ride happily for an hour or so. To avoid car sickness be sure to begin each training session at least two hours after your dog's last meal. Remember to keep pets in the back seat, so your attention will be on driving and you'll be free to handle any traffic emergency that might arise.

Dry Run

If your dog is extremely nervous about the car, you may wish to take a more gradual approach and devote the first week to simply getting him accustomed to the inside of the automobile. Begin by placing your dog in a parked car with the motor off, and all the windows and doors open. With his leash on, have him get in and out of the car several times. Then, let him sit in the back seat on a favorite blanket or towel. Try to make him feel at ease by speaking softly to him, offering him a dog treat if you wish, and lavishing praise on him for being good. The idea is to make his associations with the car pleasurable. Then with the motor running, but the car still parked, repeat this procedure.

Once your dog becomes comfortable in the parked car, try taking him for a very short drive — just down the street and back — to give him the feeling of being in motion. Continue these short spins daily, then gradually start to increase the practice time.

I've heard that when using the "dry run" approach you should precondition your dog to car travel by playing "road noise" sounds on a tape recorder. By using this approach, he would be able to listen to horns honking, cars squealing, and semi trucks barreling down the freeway before he ever leaves your driveway. This sounds pretty ridiculous to me. I can just see dog owners driving around the neighborhood, microphone hanging out the car window, in an attempt to record road noise, and then sitting in a parked car with their pet listening to the tapes. I personally prefer the "dry run" method where patience and consistency usually pay off.

Car Sickness

Some animals, particularly small puppies, whose sense of balance isn't very well developed, may have trouble with motion sickness. Car sickness often results from fear and disappears once the dog becomes accustomed to car travel. To be practical during training, spread newspaper over the seat and floor of the car. There's no need to get angry if your pet gets sick; he can't help it. If he throws up, reassure him that all is forgiven and try again the next day. Very often anxiety causes an animal to release a lot of stomach acid, and too much acid means he will eventually have to throw up. Watch for these signs of car sickness: sudden restlessness or drooling. Since fresh air helps relieve nauseous feelings, leave a car window (one in the back where the dog is) open part way. If your pet continues to get sick in the car after several weeks, it's possible that he has an inner ear imbalance, a problem that should be discussed with a veterinarian.

On occasion, even extremely well-behaved dogs may behave wildly in the car. One way to prevent your pet from ranting and raving all over your car is to teach him to ride in a carrier. Carriers are good because they make pets feel protected and give them a place to hide. When teaching the pet to ride in a carrier, employ the same gradual approaches discussed earlier. But try to let another person do the driving during initial practice trips, so that you're free to sit by your dog to pet and reassure him.

What Kind Of Car Carrier Is Best?

You have much more freedom when selecting a car carrier than you do buying an air travel carrier because there are no legal standards to be met. Carriers can be purchased from a pet store, department store, or by mail order. The correct size carrier for your dog is one that allows him room to comfortably stand, sit, turn around and lie down. Oversized models should be avoided as they tend to bump animals around too much. The walls in smaller carriers usually help make trips smoother because they give pets something to brace against.

Carriers come in a variety of materials such as cardboard, plastic, and wire. Cardboard carriers are fairly strong, offer adequate ventilation, and are suitable for short car trips. For well-traveled dogs consider a wire carrier. Wire encloses and protects while letting dogs breathe freely and see as much as possible. They also provide better air circulation than enclosed carriers, which occasionally get hot and stuffy. In addition, wire won't be damaged by wetting, chewing, or scratching. To make a carrier more cozy, place a towel or blanket on its floor, along with a soft toy or two.

Introduce your pet to his carrier in your home. Try feeding him in it with the door open or letting him sleep in it. Never put your dog in his carrier as a means of discipline or to get him out of the way when he's being a nuisance. He should quickly learn that this is his very own place of refuge where he will feel safe and secure.

Making Car Rides Joy Rides

If you're like me and occasionally want to run a little more than you want your dog to run, you may decide to leave him in the car while you do an extra mile or two. I admit this is not exactly a safe practice as a great number of pets are stolen every day from locked cars. But if you're willing to accept this responsibility and be gone only a short period of time, follow the rules below so your pet will be safe and comfortable while he waits.

1. During winter months lock your dog in the car, making absolutely certain he has adequate ventilation. Make sure he has a warm spot in which to rest. Leave him alone only if it is not too cold outside. If the weather is very cold, don't leave him in the car, even if you think you'll only be gone a short time. As stated in Chapter 4, cars retain cold, act as refrigerators, and can cause pets to literally freeze to death.

2. During the summer — and there is positively no exception to this rule — never leave your pet alone in a parked car. It doesn't matter if all the windows are down or if the car is parked in the shade, you should never consider it. On an 85° F. day the temperature in a parked car, even with all the windows partly open, can reach 102° F. in ten minutes and a blistering 120° F. in a mere half hour. Even very short exposure to temperatures this high can cause irreparable brain damage or even death.

3. Regardless of how long you'll be on the road, always bring a container of water or ice cubes. This way your dog will be sure to have a drink after your run. On longer journeys, pets may salivate heavily — particularly animals who are still getting used to car travel — which is another good reason to bring along some H_2O.

4. Let your pet relieve himself before you begin your run and before beginning a car journey. Besides indicating car sickness, sudden restlessness may mean your dog has "to go." If you think this is the case, stop the car in a convenient, safe spot, snap on a leash, and take him out. The leash will prevent your dog from running around in unfamiliar areas where he could get lost or hit by a passing car.

5. Just as we are anxious to stretch and take a break during a long car ride, so are dogs. Some become so anxious, in fact, that they try to bolt, especially if something interesting has caught their eye. Again, remember to take your dog from the car only with his leash on.

6. Most pets are content to ride in the back seat of the car. This is the best place for them because there they cannot interfere with your driving. Remember, you want to be as ready and alert as possible in case an emergency arises.

7. Don't let your dog hang out of car windows. If he does he could fall out or small objects, such as pieces of glass, rocks, or insects, could get in his eyes, causing severe damage.

8. Pet seat belts are now available in a variety of sizes. One brand, a lightweight restraint vest, adjusts to either lap or diagonal car

seat belts. This style supposedly eliminates stress points which can snap bones or cut an animal.

9. When was the last time you saw a dog hanging out the back of a pickup truck? This common practice is very dangerous, but if you must transport your dog in the rear of a truck, keep him securely tied up. Give him enough room to stretch and turn around but not enough to hang off the sides or roam around. There is a product now available called "Safe-Dog," which is a clamp-and-harness system specifically designed to secure dogs in the open bed of a pickup truck. It affords sufficient play for the animal to move about and adjusts to the movement of the vehicle while preventing access to the sides or tailgate. This is an investment well worth the money. Other alternatives include transporting your pet in a car carrier or purchasing a small riding cab which can be attached to the bed of your pickup. Although these cabs are intended to provide more space for people, they are extremely strong and normally come with upholstered interiors which make them ideal for transporting dogs.

10. If your dog goes to sleep while riding in the car, this is one of the best signs you can hope for. It indicates he is calm and comfortable in a car.

LOST DOG

Heaven forbid that you should ever lose your dog while running, but if the two of you should become separated, here's what to do.

Keep records of your dog's current rabies and license numbers as well as a clear, current photograph of him. An identification tag with your name, address, and phone number on it is a mandatory item for his collar. (A sturdy split ring rather than the standard "S" hook is best for attaching tags.) Remember, when you and your dog leave the house you want to hear the jingle of his identification tags. You might also consider having your dog tattooed and registered with the National Dog Registry, 227 Stebbins Road, Carmel, NY 10512; (914)277-4485.

What To Do If You Think Your Dog Is Lost

1. Don't wait several days or weeks for your dog to come home. Notify your local city or county animal control and/or humane shelter offices *immediately*. Check with these agencies at least every other day by phone and visit in person as often as you can. Contact as many residents as possible in the area where your dog was last seen and leave your phone number with them.

2. Design a poster to mail to people in animal agency departments you've already contacted and to post on street corners in the area where your dog was last seen. Your name, your dog's name or a reward should not be mentioned in posters or ads. Rewards often encourage dog-napping. The following wording plus a picture is recommended:

MISSING

(State color and breed type and size)

(Sex)

Finder call owner at:

(give home and work phone numbers)

If you feel you absolutely must offer a reward, word it this way: "Reward for information leading to the return of . . . ." Do not specify an amount.

3. As disheartening as it sounds, telephone the city's dead animal pick up as soon as your dog disappears and make follow-up calls and visits at least once a week.
4. Run lost dog ads in local newspapers and on radio stations.
5. Don't give up and don't stop looking.

WHICH RECREATION AREAS ARE OPEN TO DOGS

Although there are an increasing number of recreational facilities around the country closed to dogs, many do still welcome pets. Numerous public parks are open to dogs and most camping areas, national parks, national forests, and state parks allow pets. Almost all these areas have leash laws and request that owners keep their pets on designated paths or trails. Compliance with leash laws is essential, otherwise pets run the risk of getting lost or injured. Unfortunately, most public beaches don't allow dogs in the water, in picnic areas, or in any public buildings, so you may not be able to teach your dog to catch sand crabs or surf in between jogs along the seashore.

Chapter 7

EATING TO RUN

We've all heard it said enough times, "To stay healthy we must eat right and get plenty of exercise." This same statement applies to dogs. As jogging clearly gives dogs plenty of exercise, it's time to review how they should eat.

When a dog is well-fed his coat is shiny and healthy, his eyes are bright, and he has an erect carriage and happy demeanor. When poorly fed he may have gastrointestinal problems, halitosis, and/or a dry, scruffy coat. Poor nutrition often results in poor bone development and retarded growth.

Centuries ago, when a dog's food came from the prey he hunted and not from a bag or a can, there was no need to worry whether he was properly fed. Many people think the reason wild dogs ate correctly was because their diet consisted of raw meat. Consequently, they assume domestic pets should have raw meat, too. To some degree, pet food manufacturers help perpetuate this misconception by emphasizing their product's meat (or meat-by-product) content, thus implying the more meat, the better the food. Contrary to this belief, an all-meat diet is neither balanced nor healthy. It should be pointed out that carnivorous wild dogs of long ago tended to prey on plant-eating herbivores, such as rabbits and deer. These dogs ate the raw flesh of their kill as well as the vegetation-packed intestines, stomach, other internal organs, and bones. In this way they consumed a complete diet.

Today, pets are dependent on us for their nutritional needs. Fortunately, most commercial pet foods have been adequately tested and provide animals with a balanced diet. Furthermore, minimum daily requirements for dogs have been established by a subcommittee of the National Research Council (NRC). Pet food manufacturers must comply with these standards. These allowances are similar to Recommended Dietary Allowances (RDA) for humans established by the National Academy of Sciences.

Nutritional allowances for both man and animal stress the correct proportions of carbohydrates, proteins, fats, vitamins, and minerals. However,

because such allowances are based on "average" dogs, a number of factors can affect recommended canine nutritional needs. These factors include increased exercise, age, weather, stress, disease, pregnancy, and feeding habits. Besides discussing how jogging affects canine nutritional needs, each of these other factors will be analyzed individually, since active dogs can also be old or young, run in cold or hot weather, undergo stress, be pregnant, be sick, or have a change in their feeding schedule.

FACTORS AFFECTING NUTRITIONAL NEEDS

Increased Exercise — Jogging

Obviously running is likely to affect how much to feed your dog. Active dogs burn more calories than less active ones and will probably require more food. A dog running the maximum distance for his size and breed type may require up to 50 percent more calories than when he is not exercising. Most pet food manufacturers provide buyers with sufficient feeding instructions, but a general rule of thumb is: one-third to one-half ounce of dry food per pound of body weight per day. In other words, a 32-pound dog needs approximately 11 to 16 ounces, or 1 1/2 to 2 cups, of dry food daily on a maintenance diet. (Concentrated, high-protein formulas now available on the market should be fed in smaller quantities according to package directions.)

However, according to the owners of jogging dogs, increased exercise has *not* led to longer grocery lists for the pets. Duke, a five-year-old English Setter, runs more miles with his owner, Howard Kunz, than any dog I know. It's hard to believe, but Duke frequently averages 40 miles per week in the summer and 45 to 50 miles per week during the winter.

Yet he still eats one meal a day (which consists of approximately two-thirds dry food and one-third canned food).

For the most part, dogs eat only to fulfill biological needs and, as a rule, won't overeat, even when heavily exercised. Should your dog begin looking haggard, he probably needs extra food. (Note: Some breeds such

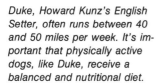

Duke, Howard Kunz's English Setter, often runs between 40 and 50 miles per week. It's important that physically active dogs, like Duke, receive a balanced and nutritional diet.

as Greyhounds and Salukis naturally present a gaunt-type appearance.) Probably more significant than how much we feed active pets is *what* they eat. But first, here's how to assess your dog's weight.

Lightly place the palms of your hands on both sides of the dog's rib cage. Make sure your hands are over his chest area and not his abdomen. With your hands properly placed you should be able to feel bone but not be able to easily feel individual ribs. On the other hand, you shouldn't have to probe deeply to detect the ribs. (Any roundness or fullness in the stomach area may indicate gas rather than fat.) This simple test can give you a quick indication of whether your dog's weight is correct. If you can "pinch an inch" of fat on the shoulders or ribs, the dog is probably overweight.

Age

Puppies require about twice as much protein and calories as adult dogs and may consume ten to fifteen percent of their weight daily. After about six months of age, this tendency should begin to decline.

As dogs age, digestion becomes more difficult and fats will need to be reduced. Just as elderly people need less food as their system slows down, older dogs, too, usually require less food.

Weather

In order to produce more body heat during cold months, dogs metabolize their food faster, thus requiring as much as 70 to 100 percent more calories per day. On the other hand, during hot weather dogs have a tendency to eat considerably less. Water should be available to them at all times, since liquids help regulate their body temperature.

Stress

Dogs can be subjected to stress in a number of ways: dog shows, disharmony in the family, a visit to a veterinarian or boarding kennel, strenuous activities such as dog sled racing or running extremely long distances, and during estrus "heat" for females or breeding season for males. Under stressful situations a caloric increase is usually necessary.

Disease

Disease or illness can deplete a dog's body of adequate nutrition. External and internal parasites, such as fleas and worms, are just a few of the "unwanted organisms" that exhaust nutrients. Parasites and disease-producing organisms are best avoided with proper feeding, care, and good sanitation.

Reproduction

Nutrition is important in maintaining fertility in both the stud dog and the brood bitch. Pregnant females use their storehouse of food and nutrients to nourish developing embryos. Over-feeding or under-feeding animals during the first weeks of gestation will increase embryo mortality. Milk production is affected by protein and fat, both of which should be abundant in the pregnant dog's diet. Consult your veterinarian for appropriate diet recommendations.

Feeding Habits

Dogs are creatures of habit and need to be fed on a regular schedule. Such feedings keep a dog's appetite steady and bowel movements regular. All dogs should be fed individually and allowed to eat at their own pace.

If you are uncertain about what you are feeding your dog, consult a veterinarian. Review your dog's lifestyle, environment, temperament, weight, age, and any other factors that might affect his appetite. Ask advice on quality and amounts of food to feed.

HOW TO ANALYZE YOUR DOG'S FOOD

Fuel for muscular work is obtained from carbohydrates, fats, or proteins. A balanced canine diet consists of sixty-seven percent carbohydrates, twenty-two percent protein, and five to ten percent fat. Man, by contrast, needs sixty-five percent carbohydrates, twenty-two to thirty percent digestible protein, and ten to twelve percent fat. Proteins are often overemphasized for both man and animal; it is actually carbohydrates that supply both species with the greatest amount of energy. It is no wonder, then, that runners indulge in "carbo-loading" and spaghetti dinners several days before a big race. These runners realize that complex carbohydrates, such as bread, potatoes, and pasta, are an athlete's best sources of energy. This is not to say that proteins aren't important — they compose about half of every cell and are crucial to cell metabolism. Additionally, proteins are important for fighting infection and promoting growth.

Because active dogs, like human marathoners, need plenty of carbohydrates, I believe these are the single most important ingredients which dog joggers should provide for their animals. Therefore, to make sure your dog is getting plenty of carbohydrates (and proteins and fats, too, for that matter) it's helpful to know how to read dog food ingredient labels. All pet food manufacturers are required by federal law to list ingredients. Typically, product labels look something like this:

Dry Dog Food		Canned Dog Food	
GUARANTEED ANALYSIS:		GUARANTEED ANALYSIS:	
CRUDE PROTEIN (MIN.)*	21%	CRUDE PROTEIN (MIN.)*	10%
CRUDE FAT (MIN.)	8%	CRUDE FAT (MIN.)	6%
CRUDE FIBER (MAX.)	4%	CRUDE FIBER (MAX.)	1%
MOISTURE (MAX.)	12%	MOISTURE (MAX.)	78%

* Note: When evaluating dog food, it is important that the protein be digestible by the dog's system. High quality meat protein is one of the best sources, followed by meat by-products.

When analyzing a brand of dog food it is necessary to convert ingredient percentages to "solid weight" percentages. Determining a product's solid weight is useful because the moisture content can vary greatly between products. Solid weights give a much more accurate picture of what's contained in a particular pet food.

In the two examples above, the dry food is only 12 percent moisture, while the canned food contains 78 percent moisture; therefore, they can't be directly compared without further analysis. If ingredient percentages are converted to solid weight figures, a more accurate comparison can be made:

1. Subtract a product's listed moisture content from 100 percent. Using the examples above, we get a solid weight of 88 percent (100 percent minus 12 percent) for the dry food and 22 percent (100 percent minus 78 percent) for the canned food.

2. Then, divide each ingredient by this new solid weight percentage number: 21 percent crude protein divided by 88 percent; 8 percent crude fat divided by 88 percent; 4 percent crude fiber (carbohydrates) divided by 88 percent. Using this formula, the new amounts we get for the previous examples are:

Dry Dog Food		Canned Dog Food	
CRUDE PROTEIN	24%	CRUDE PROTEIN	45%
CRUDE FAT	9%	CRUDE FAT	27%
CRUDE FIBER	5%	CRUDE FIBER	5%
SOLID WEIGHT	88%	SOLID WEIGHT	22%

At this point a truer comparison can begin. Without adjusting for the moisture content, it *appears* that the dry dog food contains approximately twice as much protein as the canned dog food (21 percent dry versus 10 percent canned). Just the opposite is true, however, after adjusting for moisture content (24 percent dry versus 45 percent canned).

Incidentally, many low-cost "generic" pet foods meet NRC requirements but do not always contain digestible proteins, carbohydrates, and fats. *Therefore, if you're stressing your dog by running, it becomes especially important to purchase name-brand quality pet foods that have proven research programs.*

A quick note regarding vitamins: They are essential to your dog's well-being, but are only needed in very small quantities. With a balanced diet, a vitamin deficiency shouldn't develop. Frequently, vitamin and mineral supplements are recommended for puppies, pregnant bitches, and older canines.

The consistency and color of a dog's stool tell a great deal about what is going on in the digestive system. Too soft, watery, or hard, pellet-like stools can indicate a problem. Ingested bones have a tendency to cause hard stools, which is one reason authorities recommend they be avoided. To judge, remember that stools of normal consistency can be easily picked up with a paper towel.

A change in your dog's stool color — to dark brown, black, orangish-yellow, or gray — can also signal digestive problems. Color, however, is not necessarily a bad sign, provided the dog is otherwise healthy. For example, dyed red pet foods will often color a dog's stools red. Rarely are dogs constipated — a more common cause of straining is diarrhea.

GENERAL FEEDING INFORMATION AND TIPS

1. *Feed your dog in an undisturbed place and be sure fresh, clean water is available at all times.* Because dry foods contain less moisture than canned foods (about 10 percent versus 75 percent moisture), your dog will drink more or less water accordingly. Under normal conditions, dogs need approximately 3/4 ounce of water per pound of body weight. A dog that is exercising or working, however, may require up to 75 percent more water than his sedentary companion, especially during hot weather.

2. *For dogs on a regular exercise program, two meals a day are usually recommended.* The best time for feeding is in the morning and evening. It's not wise to run your dog until two to three hours after he has finished his meal. Likewise, wait about an hour after you've run him before feeding.

3. *Don't worry if your pet wolfs down his food.* This tendency is probably a holdover from times when dogs ran with packs and had to grab their share or go hungry.

4. *Occasionally dogs will regurgitate undigested food.* This usually means a dog's digestive juices have not started to flow sufficiently to cope with the sudden intake of food. If the problem occurs frequently, however, consult your veterinarian.

5. *Every now and then your dog may skip a meal.* According to Dr. Richard Pitcairn, author of *Natural Health For Dogs & Cats* (Rodale Press), this is nothing to get alarmed about. He says it's normal for dogs not to eat every day and believes regular fasts are actually beneficial because they mimic natural conditions and give an animal's digestive tract "a chance to put aside regular duties and get to some overlooked housecleaning."

6. *Do not leave moist food (either dry mixed with water or canned) out for an extended period of time, as it will become rancid.* Normal adult dogs usually consume all the food they require each day within a ten-minute period. Leftovers should be removed and carefully covered after the animal walks away from his bowl. Store dry food in a cool place. Once opened, store canned food in the refrigerator.

7. *Contrary to popular belief, eggs are not necessarily good for dogs.* Uncooked whites destroy biotin, an important vitamin in the intestines. Only when trying to add protein to a dog's diet (check with your veterinarian first) should eggs be added, and then use only the yolks. Eggs should be offered only if they are cooked.

Chapter 8

GROOMING YOUR ACTIVE DOG

The truth I do not stretch or shove
When I state the dog is full of love.
I've also proved, by actual test,
A wet dog is the lovingest.

Ogden Nash
from *Everyone But Thee and Me*

Obviously, the more your dog runs the more opportunities he'll have to get dirty. My own dog is certainly no exception to this rule.

Willie begins each run as pristine as new-fallen snow. She's even earned such nicknames as "Snowball" and "Cottonwad." But since we live in Texas, where it seems the weather is hot ninety percent of the time, I always allow her to run through puddles and ponds. The result? Perhaps one of her other nicknames will give you a clue—"Oreo." By the end of our run her topside is relatively clean, but her legs and underside are black and covered with mud.

How do I deal with this? For one thing, I've learned to live with a certain amount of dirt and for another, I simply brush and bathe Willie more frequently. Some might say "Gee, dog jogging will be a hassle if my dog gets dirty all the time and requires constant grooming." But like me, they'll probably learn to live with the inconvenience because the pleasures of dog jogging undeniably outweigh any grooming drawbacks.

BATHING

Generally the rule is, if your dog smells "doggy," bathe him. Oils return to a dog's hair and skin within twenty-four hours, so bathing can usually be done once or twice a week or, as in my case, as often as necessary.

The following steps should help make your dog's bath time a little more bearable. Try rubbing a few drops of mineral oil over your dog's eyes to keep the soap out. Rubbing petroleum jelly over the scrotum or vulva can help prevent soap burns, and cotton balls placed in the ears can prevent water from entering. Remember to put cotton just inside the ears; putting it too far in the ears is dangerous. Place a rubber tub mat or towel in the tub to give your dog better footing. Use only warm water — never hot — and talk quietly to your pet during his bath. Remember: Try to make bathing a pleasurable and playful experience.

Shampooing

Brush and comb out any mats before bathing your dog. Combing a wet coat is almost impossible and is apt to tear out hair. Shampoo the head first. Don't use soap or shampoo meant for humans because it is probably too harsh for a dog's skin. Wash your dog's face with a sponge and clean water. Rinse him well — traces of shampoo will dry his delicate skin and cause itching. If you don't mind a wet floor, let him shake himself off. He'll do a more efficient job of getting excess water off than you can. Then dry him, using a blow dryer or towel. If the weather is cold, keep him indoors for two or three hours or until he's completely dry. Incidentally, a game of indoor towel tug-of-war or any kind of fun-and-games is a nice way to reward your pet for tolerating what he probably feels is a less than enjoyable experience.

BRUSHING/COMBING

Naturally, short-haired breeds are easier to maintain than those of the long-haired variety. But regular brushing should help reduce the need for baths, as will cleaning the mud off your dog's paws after he runs. Have your dog stand while you brush him. Use long strokes, gently brushing his fur — not his skin — in the direction it grows. It is generally recommended that short-haired breeds be combed one or two times a week with a grooming glove, a soft-to-medium bristle brush, or a fine tooth comb. Long-haired breeds need brushing as often as necessary to prevent matting, and a bristle or wire brush usually works best. For long-haired dogs, brush a handful of hair at a time.

Mats

Keep the thick tufts of hair between the toes of hairier dogs trimmed. Otherwise, burrs, stickers, or foxtails can produce feltlike mats which can be painful and cause lameness. Mats can either be cut apart with a mat splitter or scissors, or worked out gently with your fingers or a comb. Some dog groomers recommend applying a detangler, mineral oil, or olive oil to mats to make them easier to remove. Be careful when cutting mats close to the skin. A dog's skin is loose and can be easily nicked.

NAIL CARE

Running on hard surfaces such as concrete will usually keep a dog's nails worn down enough so that they won't touch the ground. A good rule to follow is if you can hear your pet's nails on a hardwood floor they're too long. Long nails can grow into the footpad and cause a dog to stand improperly. When trimming nails, stop just short of the pink area, known as the dermis, which contains nerves and blood vessels. If the nail is dark and the pink can't be seen, try using a penlight to determine where the dermis starts. Don't trim too closely or the nail will bleed. (To stop bleeding use a styptic pencil or powder, or apply direct pressure with a clean cloth.) Don't neglect the dewclaw, which grows above the paw (if your dog hasn't had them removed). Since it doesn't touch the ground, this nail may require more frequent trimming. A guillotine-type nail clipper works best for trimming all nails.

EXTERNAL PARASITES AND OTHER PROBLEMS

Ticks

Two types of ticks are most common: the Brown Dog Tick, and the American Dog Tick. The American variety is a carrier of several diseases including the often fatal Rocky Mountain Spotted Fever. Ticks can be found anywhere on the skin but they prefer the ear flaps, head, neck, shoulders, and between the toes. They bury their heads in the skin to suck blood. When removing them, care must be taken to see that the tick's mouthpiece does not remain embedded.

The best method for removal is to grasp the tick with tweezers close to where it is embedded and firmly pull it out. Soaking the tick with alcohol or nail polish remover will plug up its breathing holes and make removal easier. Burn the tick with a match after removal. A scab may form over the area where the tick was pulled out — this should not be mistaken for the tick growing back.

Fleas

A bath with a good tick and flea shampoo or dip is the most effective way to kill fleas. However, Jon Levy, an avid dog jogger, thinks he may have stumbled onto a better method of ridding dogs of fleas. If you recall, we were introduced to Jon and his two Labradors, Buck and Kate, in Chapter 1. They are long-time runners who cover a lot of neighborhood miles together each week.

Awhile back Kate had to stop running while she recovered from a non-running related operation. That's when Jon noticed she had more fleas than ever before. Buck, on the other hand, continued to run with Jon regularly and had no fleas. Previously, neither dog had been troubled by fleas and both animals slept in the same area. So why was Kate, the non-running dog, having so much trouble with these pests? Well, Jon decided it had to be the running. He suggests that perhaps running causes a dog's temperature to rise, or even changes his body chemistry in such a way that fleas no longer prefer staying on him. Although Jon jokes about his flea prevention theory, it is possible that he's onto something.

While we wait for Jon's theory to be confirmed, a good commercial powder, spray, or dip will aid in eliminating fleas. For very bad flea in-festations, your veterinarian may recommend one of the new orally ad-ministered internal insecticides. If you use a flea collar, be sure to carefully follow the manufacturer's directions. And remember, since pests thrive in hot weather, parasite control is especially important during the summer months.

Paint, Tar And Chewing Gum

Use turpentine to remove paint from your dog's body. Thoroughly clean excess turpentine off with a mild soap and water, as any residue may irritate the skin.

Nail polish remover should help take off pieces of tar and chewing gum. Again, be certain to wash this cleaner off with a mild soap and water.

"The air can be real dry here and a dog can lose tremendous amounts of water in a short period of time," cautions Arizona resident Chuck LeBenz. But with Phoenix's extensive system of canals, Pasha, Chuck's six-year-old Golden Retriever, stays refreshed as well as clean.

GROOMING DIAGNOSTICS

Grooming sessions are a convenient time to give your pet a quick check for any health problems. Call or visit your veterinarian for advice if you notice any of the following:

1. Lumps under the skin; rashes, bald spots, sores; wincing when a particular area is touched; cuts or abscesses; dull coat, flaky skin; mats, burrs, or external parasites

2. Strong ear odor; excessive or dark brown ear wax; swelling, sores

3. Tartar on teeth, mouth odor; sores or swelling in the mouth or on gums; bluish gums and tongue; foreign objects caught in teeth

4. Red, inflamed, jaundiced, runny, or cloudy eyes

5. Deep cracks on nose; nasal discharge

6. Cracked skin on paws

7. Ingrown or excessively long nails.

Chapter 9

REST AND MASSAGE

Oblige the old adage and let sleeping dogs lie. This aphorism is especially true for physically active dogs. They, just like human sportsmen, need adequate amounts of rest. Therefore, it is important to provide your dog with a cozy spot of his own, making sure it is dry, comfortable and quiet — somewhere he can get uninterrupted sleep.

Canine Heart Rate And Fatigue

Many human runners monitor their heart rate daily as a means of gauging stress. Since we've learned that a dog's body works physiologically the same as ours (see Chapter 2), we can use our pet's daily heart rate to determine whether he's getting fatigued.

To take your dog's heart rate place your fingers lightly in the middle of the upper portion of his inner thigh and count the number of beats for thirty seconds. Then, multiply this number by two. A dog's normal resting heart rate is 80 to 140 beats per minute. (By contrast, ours is about 70 to 80 beats per minute.) Early morning, before your dog becomes physically active, is the best time to take a heart rate reading. After a few weeks you will be able to estimate your pet's "norm." When his heart rate goes up more than 10 to 20 percent consider giving him an extra day of rest.

Stated previously, it's wise to follow a "hard-easy" approach when starting your dog on a running program. The hard-easy method of training allows your dog's body (and yours, too) time to catch up and avoid exhaustion. Remember: For every hard or long day of running take it easy the next day. Don't run as far or overexert yourself. Or, if you wish, take the day off completely and work out every other day. With this approach, neither you nor your dog should get too tired.

Finally, there is one other way, as ridiculous as it may sound, to help

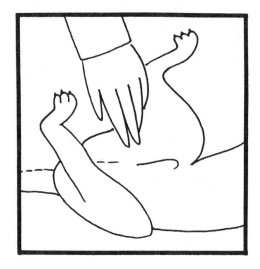

To take your dog's heart rate place your fingers lightly in the middle of the upper portion of his inner thigh.

your pet relax, and that is massage. No, you don't have to hire a Swiss masseur, you can give your pet a massage by yourself. It's easy and your pet should love it.

There are times when even internationally ranked 2:08 marathoner Dick Beardsley, of Rush City, Minnesota, has a hard time keeping up with his rambunctious pets, Samantha and Spike. Experienced long distance runners, like Dick, know the benefits of rest and usually schedule easy days between strenuous ones. (Photo by Kurt Foss/Courtesy Runner's World)

MASSAGE

Your dog's body can become sore and stiff from running just as yours can. This is why giving your dog a regular massage can be extremely beneficial — it allows you to rub out any aches and pains. Other benefits include the ability to lower your dog's heart rate and increase his circulation. It's also useful in detecting ailments that might have otherwise gone unnoticed, such as minor cuts and scrapes, parasites, and sore spots. In addition, it will undoubtedly give you a new appreciation of your pet's anatomy. But, most of all, massage is a wonderful way to strengthen the bond between you and your dog.

The best way to give a massage is on a carpeted floor with your dog either sitting or lying down. The down position is usually best for massaging your pet's hind legs. Talk to your dog in a quiet, reassuring voice while you're massaging and praise him for relaxing. Use long, firm strokes that are different from regular petting. Avoid slapping, pinching, or pulling him. If your dog thinks this is play time, let him frolic a bit, then place an open palm over his lower abdominal area for a moment. This usually has a calming effect. It may take time for your dog to get used to being touched in this new way, so be patient and start massaging the areas you know he likes rubbed. Thereafter, add one area that's sensitive.

Begin massaging your dog's head, gently moving over the eyelids, muzzle, and nose. Shift down to the neck, chest, and pectoral muscles. Try to always keep one hand in contact with your dog during the massage. Work up his forelegs, abdomen, hind legs, and then hips and back. Attempt to make contact with almost every part of his body. Thoroughly rub around the joints because strain often builds up in these areas. Take time to examine your dog's footpads and the skin between his digits. Feel his muscles and bones for anything unusual.

If you would enjoy learning more about pet massage, *The Healing Touch* by Michael Fox, D.V.M., (Newmarket Press) is an excellent resource.

Running helps "mellow him out," says Chicago resident, Peggy Gannon, of Schnapps, her Miniature Schnauzer.

The following information serves as a review of the signs of healthy and unhealthy dogs. The lists contain various overall health factors that you should regularly watch for, not just during running or massage sessions.

Healthy Signs:

First of all, the ol' nose test for determining your pet's condition — a dry-hot or moist-cold nose — is very unreliable. It's better to watch for these signs:

1. Bright eyes
2. Happy attitude and demeanor
3. Shiny coat

4. Regular appetite
5. Normal temperature (99.5 ° F. to 102.5 ° F. — average is 101.1 ° F.)
6. Normal color and consistent stool

Unhealthy Signs:

1. Behavioral changes
2. Any change in appetite that lasts more than three days
3. Urinates more or less than usual
4. Extremely high (rectal) temperature
5. Coprophagy (stool eating) — which may indicate a nutritional deficiency
6. Lameness, stiff neck, or reluctance to get up or lie down
7. Vomiting or stool with blood
8. Distended abdomen (bloatedness)
9. White or pale gums
10. Bad breath
11. Excessive loss of hair
12. Chronic cough
13. Dehydrated or excessive thirst
14. Excessive salivation
15. Excessive shaking of head

A good item to always keep around your house is an at-home veterinary care book. Dr. Sheldon L. Gerstenfeld's *Taking Care of Your Dog* (Addison-Wesley Publishing Co.) is one of the easiest medical guides to read and to follow.

Chapter 10

FIRST AID. . . JUST IN CASE

Hopefully you'll never have to administer first aid to your pet while jogging, or at any other time for that matter. But accidents do happen, and knowledge of what to do can be most reassuring.

Ohio native Laurie Pipenur always reserves mornings for her two frisky Dalmatians, Daisy and Tucker. Together they run a three-mile neighborhood course which is jam-packed with the kinds of "prey" that capture the dogs' attention: cats, squirrels, lawn sprinklers, garbage bags, and tree stumps. To avoid being dragged into every front yard or knocked clean off her feet (which has happened more than once), Laurie has learned to anticipate these objects in advance and keep a good, strong grip on the dogs' leashes. Trying to hold back two large, powerful, very intent Dalmatians, she says, "is like trying to rein wild horses." Sometimes even all the strength she can muster is not enough to do the job.

During one recent morning run, all was going well until one of the dogs discovered a dead rat in the road. Seconds later, both dogs went for it. Laurie screamed "No!" at the top of her lungs, which convinced only Tucker to back away from the rat. In the meantime, Daisy devoured it. Panic-stricken, Laurie made for home with the dogs, terrible "what-if" thoughts filling her mind. "What if the rat had eaten poison?" "What if it had rabies?" Not knowing what to do, she called the dogs' breeder and handler, who recommended giving Daisy two tablespoons of hydrogen peroxide. Vomiting was induced within minutes, and after a good rest Daisy was fine.

Although the chances of your dog eating a dead animal while jogging are slim, Laurie Pipenur's story points out how easily the unexpected can happen. Incidentally, although Laurie's first reaction was to call her breeder (who, luckily, is very knowledgeable about such health matters), your dog's veterinarian is really the one to call in an emergency.

Dalmatians, Daisy and Tucker enjoy giving Laurie Pipenur a good workout when they run.

GETTING PREPARED

"Hurry up, I know the bandages are in there somewhere." "Let's see, where did I put the veterinarian's emergency phone number?" "Uh-oh, Sparky's not breathing too well. What should I do?" One of the best ways to remain calm during an emergency is to be prepared. Assembling a first aid kit for your dog ensures that everything is in one place when the need arises.

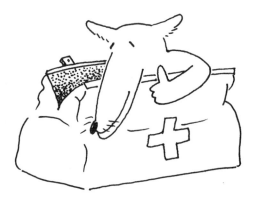

Your Pet First Aid Kit

The first item to include in your pet's first aid kit is a card with several veterinary clinics and emergency phone numbers; the telephone number and address of the closest 24-hour emergency animal clinic just in case a veterinarian is unavailable (it's a good idea to keep these same telephone numbers in your wallet, sportsbag, and/or the glove box of your car); and your dog's birthdate, average weight, normal temperature, vaccination history, and medical history. Here's what else belongs in the kit:

Hydrogen Peroxide (3 percent solution)—To clean wounds or induce vomiting.

Rectal Thermometer—A dog's normal body temperature varies from 99.5° F. to 102.5° F. and usually averages about 101° F.

Petroleum Jelly—To lubricate the thermometer.

Betadine Solution—A non-stinging iodine for wounds.

Gauze Pads or Clean Cloths—To protect wounds and burns, and control bleeding.

Gauze Roll—For wrapping wounds or muzzling an injured animal.

Adhesive Tape (1-inch wide roll)—To secure bandages.

Buffered Aspirin or Baby Aspirin*—For pain and fever.

Neosporin Ointment—Disinfectant for burns and scrapes.

Pepto-Bismol Liquid*—To control vomiting and stomach upsets.

Kaopectate*—To control diarrhea.

Milk of Magnesia*—To control constipation.

Tweezers—For removal of splinters or glass.

Plastic Eyedropper or Hypodermic Syringe (3 ml, 5 ml, or 10 ml depending on the size of the dog and anticipated dosage)—To aid in giving liquid medicine.

Scissors—To clip hair around wounds, or cut gauze, tape, etc.

Clean Newspaper—To be rolled up as a makeshift splint.

Check dosages with veterinarian before administering to pet.

Now that you're prepared for medical emergencies, let's review some commonplace canine catastrophes. Knowledge of what to do in the following situations will help you care for your dog swiftly and responsibly.

HOW TO MUZZLE A DOG

When frightened and in pain, dogs may not recognize their owners and may try to bite. Therefore, it's advisable to first muzzle the animal before administering first aid. Ideally, a gauze strip two-and-one-half feet long or

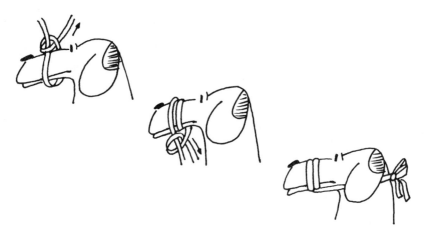

cloth strip one inch wide should be used. However, any available substitute, such as a cloth belt, leash, piece of rope, necktie, or shoelace, will work. Be sure to approach the dog slowly and quietly, and speak to him in a comforting voice.

Tie a loose knot in the middle of the bandage or cloth, making a large loop. Slip this loop on your dog's muzzle, about two-thirds of the way from nose tip to jaw. Don't worry, this procedure will not affect the dog's breathing or hurt him. Now, knot the loop securely on top, then again below the nose, and tie the two ends behind the dog's head. Note: Do not muzzle a dog that is vomiting or choking.

TRANSPORTING AN INJURED DOG

To support a small or medium size dog, place your inner right arm under his rear with your inner left arm under his chest. His side should be placed against your chest and his legs hanging free, much like you'd carry a big stereo speaker. Large or giant breeds should be carried by two people when possible. One person supports the chest while the other supports the rear and abdomen. If you're alone, stoop down with your back toward the dog, put him on your shoulders, and hold his feet in front. If the dog is conscious, muzzle him so he won't be able to bite your face in his pain and confusion. A car mat, blanket, or even your jacket can be

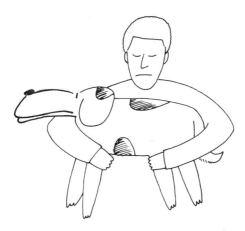

used as a stretcher when transporting a seriously injured dog. Try not to change the dog's position when sliding him on a stretcher. Note: Do not lift or rotate your pet if he is in shock or suffering abdominal or limb injuries.

SHOCK

Canine shock occurs when a dog suffers a severe trauma — such as being hit by a car or blood loss from a deep cut — causing the circulatory system to slow down and become incapable of supplying the body tissues, especially the brain, with enough oxygen to remain alive. Possible symptoms of shock include:

- Pale gums - Test by pressing your finger to the gum. Normally it will turn pink after a few seconds, but when a dog is in shock it turns white.
- Glassy eyes - Caused by dilation of the pupils.
- Rapid heartbeat - Over 140 beats per minute.
- Shallow breathing.
- A bewildered appearance.

Dogs in shock should be kept as quiet as possible; avoid noise and loud talk which might prompt him to move. If it is cold outside, keep the dog warm by covering his body with a blanket or jacket. Try to keep the dog's head lower than his hindquarters by slightly elevating the legs; this way blood can get to the brain which may prevent brain damage. If his breathing is troubled, begin artificial respiration (see below). Dogs suffering from shock should be taken to a veterinarian as soon as possible, since the administration of intravenous fluids and drugs may mean the difference between life and death.

BREATHING PROBLEMS (ARTIFICIAL RESPIRATION)

Should your dog have trouble breathing or stop breathing complete-ly, lay him on his side and check the mouth for obstructions by pulling out his tongue so that you can see deep into the throat. To ensure a clean air passage, remove any blood or mucus with your fingers or a towel. Then hold the dog's mouth closed to form a seal and cover your mouth over his nose. Breathe into the nose until the chest expands. Remove your mouth and let the chest fall. Repeat this step, giving ten to fifteen breaths per minute. Once the dog is breathing on his own, immediately take him to the veterinarian.

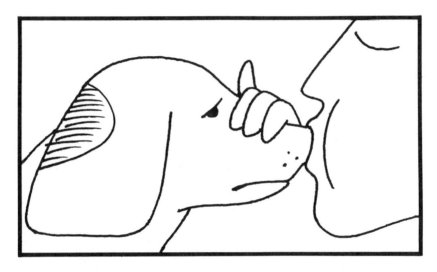

CAR ACCIDENTS

If not the country's leading canine killer, automobiles certainly are the leading cause of injury. The best way to prevent such accidents is to avoid cars. Don't run along heavily traveled roads or with your dog off leash. If your dog does get hit by a car, restrain him with a leash or belt; if he has no difficulty breathing, muzzle him if necessary. DO NOT use a muzzle if bloody bubbles are coming from the nostrils or if you suspect internal bleeding. Apply pressure with your hand, gauze pad, or ice pack to any superficial wounds and then bandage if necessary. If the wound is large and bleeding is excessive, apply pressure to the bleeding area, restrict motion, and see a veterinarian as soon as possible. Cover your dog with a blanket if he is in shock (see symptoms listed on page 89). If you suspect that a bone is broken, apply a splint (see illustration on page 92) and transport the animal to a veterinarian using a blanket or a piece of wood as a stretcher.

BLEEDING

Apply direct pressure to the wound with your hand or use a pressure bandage. If first aid materials are handy, place a gauze pad over the wound, use gauze strips to wrap it tightly, and tie or tape the ends. If this fails to stop or dramatically slow the bleeding, apply a tourniquet, but do so only as a last resort. A tourniquet can cause loss of limb or nerve damage if left in place too long.

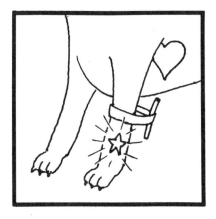 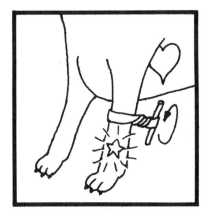

To make a tourniquet, wrap gauze, fabric, or rope twice around the extremity, between the heart and the wound, and knot it. *Do not make the tourniquet too tight.* See a veterinarian immediately. If a veterinary facility is more than fifteen to twenty minutes away, loosen the tourniquet every five minutes.

CUTS

Cuts on footpads occur less frequently than one might think. Dogs usually are good about sidestepping sharp and jagged objects that can cut their footpads. Smaller cuts, whether on a dog's foot or elsewhere on the body, usually stop bleeding on their own in about five minutes. If the wound is large, apply direct pressure with a clean cloth, towel, or gauze pad for five to ten minutes, then release pressure to allow the blood to clot. After the bleeding stops, use scissors to clip hair from around the cut and clean the wound with soap and water. Hydrogen peroxide (three percent solution) may also be used. Do not rub the wound hard or the clot may loosen and cause the bleeding to recur. Place a gauze pad or clean cloth over the wound and wrap snugly with a gauze roll or cloth strips and tape. Replace bandage daily. See your veterinarian as soon as possible if bleeding is uncontrollable, and/or if the cut requires stitches. Should the wound exhibit signs of infection, definitely seek veterinary advice.

LAMENESS, SPRAINS, AND FRACTURES

Lameness can be caused by a number of problems. A dog can twist his leg by stepping into a hole or onto foreign objects, such as thorns or glass. A lame front leg will cause a dog's head to bob up when that leg touches the ground, while a lame rear leg will cause the head to bob down. Dogs usually display a shorter stride and lighter touch when they have a sore leg. Tar and paint, which may cause soreness, can be removed by wrapping the paw in a bandage soaked with mineral oil or vegetable oil for twelve to twenty-four hours. After removing the soaked bandage, wash the affected area with soap and water. Thorns or other sharp objects can be removed from the paw with your fingers or tweezers. If lameness grows worse or lasts longer than three days, see a veterinarian.

Sprains and fractures oftentimes cannot be discovered with the eye or by hand. A sprain, less severe than a fracture, occurs when the tissues that connect bones are torn. Fractures (broken bones) should be suspected (and X-rayed) when a dog does not bear weight on a limb, has a crooked leg, bone protruding through the skin, or pain and swelling.

Follow these steps for treating fractured bones that do not protrude through the skin:

1. Make a splint out of a piece of wood or folded newspaper. Place a clean cloth around the limb for padding. Tape the splint to the outside of the leg, allowing it to overlap about six inches at each end of the break.

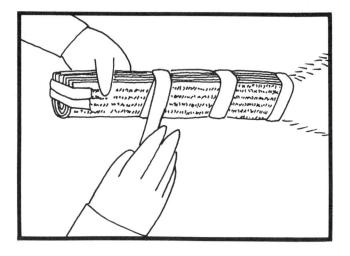

2. Tape splint securely. Make it snug, but not so tight as to cause the leg to swell.

3. See a veterinarian as soon as possible.

For fractured bones protruding through the skin:

1. Prevent the dog from licking the wound.

2. Bandage the limb if possible and make a splint (see 1 and 2 above). Frequently, the shape of a dog's leg or its resistance to handling when injured make it impossible to apply a temporary splint. In this case, gently support the limb with a towel, blanket, or board.

3. See a veterinarian immediately.

SWALLOWED OBJECTS

One may wonder if dogs have brains programmed by the Hoover Vacuum Company, what with the way they're able to gobble up foreign objects. You name it, and at one time or another some dog has undoubtedly tried to eat it. Sticks, stones, bone slivers, rubber balls, socks, shoes, trash, and marbles probably account for ninety percent of the things swallowed, which cause dogs to cough and choke, paw at their muzzles, or shake their heads. Persistent vomiting, another symptom, may indicate that some foreign object is lodged in the intestinal tract. Contact a veterinarian immediately if this occurs.

When checking for swallowed objects, examine the top and under portions of the dog's tongue, gums, teeth, and especially the roof of the mouth, where a short piece of bone or a stick can become easily lodged. Examine the throat by pulling the tongue out — use a napkin or towel for a better grip. If you see the object in the throat area and it is not too deeply imbedded, try removing it. Vomiting may be induced if the object is soft (such as a small rubber ball) or hard and smooth (like marbles). Do not induce vomiting when sharp objects have been swallowed.

CHOKING

When a dog begins choking, push the lower jaw open and tilt the head up. Using extreme caution, try to remove the object with your fingers. If you're unsuccessful, kneel behind the dog, holding the body just below the ribs, and squeeze the body hard a few times, pressing up. If the object does not pop out, rush him to the veterinarian.

CARDIOPULMONARY RESUSCITATION (CPR)

Cardiopulmonary resuscitation (CPR) is necessary if the dog's heart stops because of an accident, electrocution, or near drowning. With the dog on his side, place the heel of one of your hands on his chest, and put your other hand palm-down on top of the first hand. Press firmly, release, pause, and repeat twenty or thirty times a minute. Take care not to bruise or break the ribs. When the heartbeat resumes, see a veterinarian immediately.

DROWNING

Hold your dog upside down for ten to fifteen seconds and listen for a heartbeat. Give CPR (see above paragraph) and/or artificial respiration if there's no heartbeat. Wrap your dog warmly and take him to a veterinarian for examination.

POISONS

When a dog has ingested poison and it can be identified, the veterinarian may recommend an antidote or instruct the owner to induce vomiting with a hydrogen peroxide solution, syrup of ipecac, or other emetic. Do not induce vomiting unless you're sure of what was swallowed. (With some poisons it's harmful to induce vomiting.) It's sometimes easier to give liquid medicine with an eyedropper. Pull the dog's lips aside at the cheek to form a pouch, and fill it with the medicine or hydrogen peroxide. Rub the dog's nose lightly — this encourages him to lick his nose, which in turn causes him to swallow the medicine. To help absorb poison, give the dog activated charcoal, milk, egg whites, or milk of magnesia if you cannot contact medical experts. Get to a veterinarian as quickly as possible.

FISHHOOKS

When careless people leave fishhooks around beaches, docks, or campgrounds, dogs are liable to end up with one in their foot or mouth. With a pair of pliers, cut off the barbed end of the hook so that it can be pulled through, or if it's more convenient, cut off the eye end so that you don't have to pull the barb back through the skin. Apply antiseptic and gauze to the wound.

BEE AND WASP STINGS

Remove the stinger with tweezers and apply baking soda and/or an ice pack to the sting site. Keep a close watch on your pet for about two hours after the sting takes place. If swelling worsens or if restlessness, vomiting, diarrhea, or difficulty in breathing occurs, or if the animal collapses, see a veterinarian at once.

SKUNKS

Running with your dog off leash in skunk country — along country roads or nature trails — could result in an odorous situation. Many inquisitive dogs have been sprayed by a skunk on the defensive. To tackle this problem, put on a pair of rubber gloves before you begin deodorizing your pet. Wash the entire body with soap and water and the eyes with plain warm water. A few drops of warm olive oil can be put in the eyes to relieve any stinging caused by the spray. Towel-dry your dog, then, using the time-honored method, wash him in tomato juice. Diluted lemon juice can also be added to cut the odor. Repeat this process as often as necessary to counteract the odor. The bathing may not take it away entirely, but it will help.

SNAKEBITES (Poisonous)

To tell if your dog has been bitten by a poisonous snake look for rapid swelling and fang marks. Snakebites usually occur on the face or legs. Treat by applying ice packs to the bite site. For leg bites, apply a compression-type bandage, being careful not to completely cut off the circulation. See your veterinarian as soon as possible.

PORCUPINE QUILLS

Running your dog off leash in the country can lead to all kinds of trouble, especially if you allow him to wander out of your sight. If your dog meets up with a porcupine, take him to a veterinarian immediately. Quills tend to work their way deeper into tissue as time goes on.

If veterinary help is not available, work the quills out yourself as soon as possible. Two people may be required to hold the dog, as this is a painful ordeal. If you are alone, grip the dog between your legs and cut off the quill tips at an angle. This releases the pressure (porcupine quills are hollow) and makes the quills easier to remove. Vinegar may also be applied to soften the quills. Gradually twist out — do not yank — each quill with a pair of pliers. Begin in the chest area, otherwise quills may work deeper through the skin and enter the vital organs. Next work on quills around the face. Apply a standard antiseptic to the wounds and get the dog to a veterinarian as soon as you can. The veterinarian may administer an anesthetic to complete what would otherwise be a long and painful process.

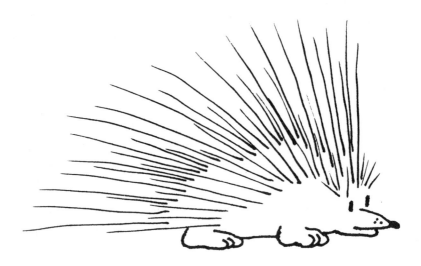

As I have stated throughout this book, I believe dog jogging is one of the most pleasurable ways to spend time with your dog, because running allows each of you to play together. According to renowned author and pet specialist Dr. Michael Fox, "Knowing how to play with your pet can break the species barrier. . . .Once this barrier is broken, man and animal can enjoy each other and so establish a depth of relationship that is rewarding and fulfilling for both."

When asked why she likes to run with Blu, Debbi Warner replies, "Companionship," but quickly adds, "and because he enjoys it so much."

Appendix

OBEDIENCE BASICS

A dog unfamiliar with obedience commands can be a demon on a run. An obedience-trained dog, on the other hand, is a joy to jog with. *Combining firmness with kindness is the key to obedience success.* A consistent tone of voice is also essential. One person should do the training, and it's important for the individual to use the same commands in the same way each time.

Obedience training for puppies can begin as soon as there is an established rapport between dog and owner. Limit training sessions to ten minutes and stop at the first sign of loss of interest. For adult dogs, longer training sessions, up to twenty minutes, are advised. Try to work with either puppies or adult dogs on a *daily* basis.

Most dogs are anxious to please their owners and a harsh tone of voice is usually a sufficient reprimand. Keep a dog's temperament in mind — is he timid or dominant by nature — and match punishment accordingly. A severe shaking is one of the most effective ways to let your dog know you really mean business; never use a stick or your hand to strike the dog. A dog understands he's done something wrong when his tail begins to droop or his ears flatten against the head.

When you are happy with your pet's behavior, praise him immediately. Be lavish with praise, make a big fuss over him, and he'll be anxious to please again.

Do obedience work with a choke collar. Select one that is large enough to fit over your dog's head, but does not allow more than one and one-half to two inches of slack around the neck. To make sure you have put the collar on correctly, think of placing a sideways "P" around your dog's neck. Corrections are then issued by making a *short, quick* jerk on the lead.

Heel

Obedience is a step-by-step process and the three most important commands are "Heel," "Come," and "Sit." To heel, your dog must learn to stay close to your left side, neither in front or behind, and follow at your pace. When jogging, you may wish to instruct your dog to heel slightly out from your left side, so you both have plenty of space for foot movement. The command "Side" or "Position" can be used instead of "Heel" when you want your dog heeling a few feet out from your left side. Start by calling the dog's name and then say "Heel" or "Side." If the dog pulls in front, jerk the lead sharply, pulling your hand back as you repeat the command. Praise him when he returns to your side.

Come

Call your dog by name and then say "Come." Tug the lead, if necessary, to encourage him to come. Praise him generously when he has obeyed.

Sit

Walk your dog, then stop and say "Sit." Pull up on the lead, keeping it taut as you bend down and press your dog's rump down. Slowly rise, keeping the lead tense, then let it slack and praise the dog.

Down

Start with the dog in a sitting position. Give the command "Down" and pull down on the lead. If this fails, pull the dog down using his collar. If this still fails, gently press down and slightly to the side on his shoulder as you pull his front legs out to bring him to a down. He should remain in this position for a minute or two until you release him with "Okay" or "Free."

Stay

Start with the dog in a sitting position. Give the command "Stay" and then slowly move away facing the dog. Say "Stay" again and back away for ten seconds. If the dog attempts to get up, put him back in a sitting position. Extend the stay time only if the dog remains in place.

Curbing

City joggers will make many friends if they teach their dog to defecate in the street. When your dog wants to "go," guide him to the street, only if there is no traffic, and say such words as "Hurry Up." When he's performed, praise him.

RECOMMENDED READING

General Books:

Fox, Michael W.
  The Healing Touch
  New York: Newmarket Press, 1981

Fox, Michael W.
  Understanding Your Dog
  New York: Bantam Books, 1974

Gerstenfeld, Sheldon L.
  Taking Care Of Your Dog
  Reading: Addison Wesley, 1982

Milani, Myrna M.
  The Weekend Dog
  New York: Rawson Associates, 1984

Monks of New Skete
  How To Be Your Dog's Best Friend
  Boston: Little, Brown, 1978

Pitcairn, Richard H. and Pitcairn, Susan H.
  Dr. Pitcairn's Complete Guide to Natural Health For Dogs And Cats
  Emmaus: Rodale Press, 1982

Rutherford, Clarice, and Neil, David
  How to Raise A Puppy You Can Live With
  Loveland: Alpine Publications, 1981

Running Guides

Beginning

Glover, Bob and Shepherd, Jack
  The Runner's Handbook
  New York: Penguin Books, 1978
Henderson, Joe
  Jog, Run, Race
  Mountain View: Anderson World, 1978

Advanced

Henderson, Joe
  Run Farther, Run Faster
  New York: Macmillan Publishing, 1984

Lawrence, Allan and Scheid, Mark
  The Self-Coached Runner
  Boston: Little, Brown, 1984

ABOUT THE AUTHOR

Davia Gallup is Founder and Race Director of the Annual Houston K-9 Fun Run, which is the largest event of its kind in the world. She hopes that one day K-9 Fun Runs will occur around the nation so every dog owner will have an opportunity to enjoy the fun and excitement of running with their dog in an organized event.

Her enthusiasm for dog jogging developed five years ago when she first began running with her dog. Gradually her interest in the effect of jogging on dogs grew and she began researching the subject, which led to the development of this book. Simultaneously, her interest in casual jogging grew until today Davia is an accomplished runner with numerous awards in track and field and road race competitions. She has competed in four marathons, including the prestigious Boston Marathon, and is most proud of her 36-minute 10K.

Gallup presently owns a public relations and marketing company in the Houston area. A native Californian, she was educated at the University of California at Berkeley, comes from a large family, and grew up with a variety of pets. Cats, dogs, rabbits, parakeets, hamsters, fish, and even an occasional snake and tarantula are just some of the animals she and her family enjoyed caring for.

Readers who would like to learn more about dogs in general, dog training, breeding, or showing, are referred to the following Alpine titles:

How to Raise a Puppy You Can Live With
Rutherford & Neil $6.98
The puppy owner's "Dr. Spock." Takes the puppy from birth to one year. 126 pgs., paper.

Best Foot Forward
Handler $5.98
Handling tips to help obedience competitors. 112 pgs., paper.

Canine Reproduction
Holst, DVM $17.98
A complete guide to canine reproduction, breeding, and whelping. 226 pgs., cloth.

Canine Hip Dysplasia and Other Orthopedic Diseases
Lanting $12.98
How to detect, treat, and prevent this disabling disease. 212 pgs:, cloth.

What's Bugging Your Dog, A Guide to Canine Parasitology
Schneider $5.98
Protect your dog's health by ridding him of external and internal parasites. 60 pgs., paper.

Scent—Training Your Dog to Track
Pearsall and Verbruggen $14.98
Enjoy the sport of tracking. An interesting scientific approach. 226 pgs., cloth.

Max, The Dog That Refused to Die
Wayne $8.98
Inspiring story of a lost Doberman Pinscher's fight for life. 70 pgs., cloth.

To order the above books, or to request our latest catalog which includes breed books and many more titles, write:

Alpine Publications, Inc.
214 Nineteenth St. S.E.
Loveland, CO 80537

Enclose check or money order or use your Master Card or Visa account. All books shipped postpaid book rate.